A Teacher's Guide to Philosophy for Children

A Teacher's Guide to Philosophy for Children provides educators with the process and structures to engage children in inquiring as a group into 'big' moral, ethical and spiritual questions, while also considering curricular necessities and the demands of national and local standards.

Based on the actual experiences of educators in diverse and global classroom contexts, this comprehensive guide gives you the tools you need to introduce philosophical thinking into your classroom, curriculum and beyond. Drawing on research-based educational and psychological models, this book highlights the advantages gained by students who regularly participate in philosophical discussion: from building cognitive and social/emotional development, to becoming more informed citizens. Helpful tools and supplementary online resources offer additional frameworks for supporting and sustaining a higher level of thinking and problem-solving among your students.

This practical guide is essential reading for teachers, coaches and anyone wondering how you can effectively teach philosophy in your classroom.

Keith J. Topping is Professor at the University of Dundee, UK.

Steven Trickey is Scholar in Residence at American University, USA.

Paul Cleghorn is an education consultant at Aude Education, UK.

A Teacher's Guide to Philosophy for Children

Keith J. Topping, Steven Trickey
and Paul Cleghorn

Routledge
Taylor & Francis Group

NEW YORK AND LONDON

First published 2019
by Routledge
52 Vanderbilt Avenue, New York, NY 10017

and by Routledge
2 Park Square, Milton Park, Abingdon, Oxon, OX14 4RN

*Routledge is an imprint of the Taylor & Francis Group,
an informa business*

Library of Congress Cataloging-in-Publication Data
A catalog record for this title has been requested

ISBN: 978-1-138-39327-1 (hbk)
ISBN: 978-1-138-39326-4 (pbk)
ISBN: 978-0-429-40187-9 (ebk)

Typeset in Sabon
by Cenveo® Publisher Services

Visit the eResources: www.routledge.com/9781138393264

Contents

Dedication and Acknowledgements

We would like to dedicate this book to Matthew Lipman, who did so much to highlight the need for independent rational thinking and who, with others, succeeded in creating a practical and liberating process for encouraging young people toward this outcome.

Thanks particularly to my wife, Doris, who brought much from her practical experience of P4C to help refine the Thinking Through Philosophy approach and build supporting classroom aids. She has also worked tirelessly when training teachers and endured many difficult conditions (particularly in rural India) in order to make this pedagogy available to all. Her help and support have been invaluable. Thanks to Jane Craik, school principal in Scotland, who has worked hard over many years to make P4C available to many teachers and schools. She represents all those who work so hard because they believe in this work and approach. Lastly, thanks to Education Renaissance Trust (London) and Yojana Projecthulp (Netherlands), who sponsored the projects in Grenada and India because they too believe in working to improve education for young people, wherever they may be.

Paul Cleghorn

I would like to thank Keir Bloomer, Director of Education for Clackmannanshire Council in Scotland when the Thinking Through Philosophy project was initiated, without whose educational vision and support that development would not have happened. I would also like to acknowledge the contributions of all colleagues in Clackmannanshire who helped with the Thinking Through Philosophy project – helping children become more penetrating and diligent in their thinking.

Steve Trickey

To my new grandson. May he grow to be wise.

Keith J. Topping

1

Introducing Thinking Through Philosophy

In their classic 1980 text on Philosophy for Children, Lipman, Sharp and Oscanyon wrote on behalf of a child: 'When I entered the educational system, I brought curiosity and imagination and creativity with me. Thanks to the system, I have left all these behind'[1] (p. 5).

This comment is stark and pessimistic, but it does raise the question of how young students can be supported to retain their curiosity and interest throughout their educational experiences while also being encouraged to be reflective and judicious in their thinking. Matthew Lipman and his colleagues developed the Philosophy for Children (P4C) program in the 1960s and 1970s. P4C has endured while many other educational initiatives have come and gone. The process of Philosophy for Children is now practiced in over 60 countries throughout the world[2].

But Lipman was not the first. Much of the questioning in P4C comes from Socratic dialogue and argument, fostered in ancient Greece. Bronson Allcott (father of Louisa May) was a schoolmaster in Boston in the 1840s and a friend and mentor to New England philosophers Emerson and Thoreau. He used a very similar questioning technique, and the sessions were recorded by a Miss Peabody, sitting in the corner! The stimuli were biblical quotations, but the discussions were fascinating and quite open. It was a bit too ahead of its time for the good folk of Boston, who closed the school down after three years.

A Teacher's Guide to Philosophy for Children aims to support teachers who want to engage their students in meaningful discussion to construct knowledge and understanding, rather than seeing learning as a repetitive process aimed at 'ticking off' narrow prescribed targets. More active engagement is likely to satisfy and fulfill the psychological needs of both learner and teacher. This book is about a method of inquiry that can be used with students of all ages to explore the meaning of difficult-to-define concepts – such as beauty, fairness and truth – and embed that knowledge in a wider context of understanding. Inquiry stimulates students (and the teacher) to think more deeply and 'reasonably' about concepts and issues in general, not just those with a philosophical dimension.

This book will provide guidance as to how this can be done. It aims to promote critical, creative and collaborative thinking and can support learning throughout the curriculum. Philosophical inquiry is also conducive to students' social and emotional development. Apart from these pragmatic reasons, engaging students in thinking together about questions that interest them is an enjoyable and motivating experience for all concerned.

Philosophy for Children aims to teach children to think for themselves and make informed choices. It also seeks to improve children's reasoning abilities and judgment by having them think about their thinking as they discuss concepts of importance to them. The process encourages children to develop critical reasoning and creative thinking skills through collaborative dialogue facilitated by their teacher. This book will consider how teachers can facilitate regular practice of Philosophy for Children so it engages students of all ages to think and inquire together. When students are able to think together, they can create meaning and extend understanding beyond that which they could achieve individually. The whole is greater than the sum of the parts. This book will also consider how P4C can promote long-term cognitive and social development.

A Teacher's Guide to Philosophy for Children provides teachers and students with a structure for exploring 'big' moral, ethical and spiritual questions such as 'What is fairness?' 'What is beauty?' or 'What is a friend?' Children are curious. It is often said that children are natural philosophers. They ask questions to make sense of the world. These questions motivate and stimulate them to look further into problems and issues. And curiously, the questions also develop the individuals into better independent learners.

Philosophical inquiries involve a search for meaning, truth, understanding and values supported by reasons. Sometimes likened to a jury, the children become seasoned inquirers and accomplished at arriving at judicious results. Such skills can be applied to the in-depth exploration of historical, literary and religious concepts – and just about any subject matter that merits learning and understanding. Philosophical inquiry is not an *exchange* of opinions but provides a context where students of all ages are challenged to *justify* their opinions. Student-led inquiry builds confidence by making space for students to create meaning from their own experience. Student motivation increases because investigating answers to their own questions has personal significance to them.

As well as exploring questions generated by the inquirers themselves (or sometimes their teacher), the practice of Philosophy for Children raises broader questions about its place in contemporary education and, for that matter, what contemporary education should be about. The methods and practices discussed in this book are based on evidence (see later chapters). *A Teacher's Guide to Philosophy for Children* connects the process of inquiry to what we know about cognitive development and learning.

Teachers are likely to be preoccupied with how they can find 'inquiry' time. In view of this, consideration is given to practical options as to how teachers set up inquiries that interest their students. For example, a school may wish P4C to sit within a particular curricular area (English, religious and moral education, social studies, form period, etc.). In some cases, a teacher can make that choice, but note that time also can be created through a more effective teaching method. This book is written by authors who have a wealth of experience in facilitating inquiries, developing philosophical initiatives, working closely with schools and educational districts, applying educational psychology in the classroom and disseminating educational and research expertise. The authors' four-year longitudinal project provided a unique opportunity to work closely with teachers in 'real' classrooms (i.e., full-size classes of up to 30 mixed-ability children), testing the scope for promoting reasoning abilities.

For Whom Is This Book Written?

A Teacher's Guide to Philosophy for Children is written for a wide audience, but the main audience is likely to consist of in-service and pre-service teachers and professional development educators. It will be relevant to researchers in this area. It will also be of value to philosophers who wish to work with schools to facilitate inquiries with children. The book will interest anyone committed to developing educational practice and passionate about actively engaging learners and enhancing emotional intelligence. The focus will be on how teachers can establish classroom contexts that support engaging students of all ages to inquire together to develop their thinking. The precious time used to facilitate weekly inquiry will be advantageous to both students and teacher. As Gregory[3] suggested, teachers bring advantages to the role of facilitator of children's philosophical dialogue. Teachers are skilled in classroom management, know their students and can make connections to other curricular areas.

Clarifying the Term 'Philosophy for Children'

Strictly speaking, 'Philosophy for Children' refers to the program developed in the United States by Mathew Lipman and his colleagues. However, a wide range of subsequent developments and materials were inspired by that program, some of which were adapted to the needs of different cultures and times.

Lipman's program focuses on reasoning and inquiry. Lipman's Philosophy for Children can be introduced at the five- to seven-year-old level and continue to around the age of sixteen years. The assumption is that children are capable of critical and reflective thinking even at a young age. The original version of Philosophy for Children comprised seven novels with corresponding support materials and training for teachers. The instruction manuals provided discussion plans to help teachers lead discussion strategically without having to wonder constantly what to say next. The central characters in the stories learned to resolve their problems through their powers of reasoning. The novels stimulated reasoned debate by raising issues such as saluting the American flag (which of course makes them culturally specific).

Some practitioners have subsequently used the term 'Philosophy *with* Children' to emphasize the collaborative nature of inquiry and the role of students in generating questions and ideas stemming from those questions. The notion that the method is only for children and therefore unnecessarily age restrictive has led to the term being expanded by some to '*Philosophy for Children, Colleges and Communities*'[2].

In this book we will use 'Philosophy for Children' in a looser sense and draw distinctions with other methods, such as *Community of Philosophical Inquiry* (CoPI)[4]. CoPI appears to place more emphasis on facilitators learning about philosophical traditions to prepare them for their role in facilitating inquiries. This contrasts with the view[3] shared by the authors that adults without academic philosophical training are capable of leading philosophical inquiries. The need for academic philosophical training also contrasts with the idea[5] of teachers 'learning on the job with support'. This book is consistent with the latter position.

Following the publication of Lipman's original materials, a wide range of alternative stimulus materials have been tailored to the needs of different groups. Alternatives to the original materials included Robert Fisher's series of books[6] that proved popular with British teachers. In Australia, Phil Cam's[7] *Thinking Together*' was widely used. In Scotland, one of the current authors, Paul Cleghorn[8], developed the *Thinking Through Philosophy* program. A steady stream of materials for supporting inquiry has continued to evolve, many attuned to different cultures, traditions and student needs. Such materials include stories, poems, pictures, media news reports, objects and moral dilemmas, all of which can used to stimulate questioning and conceptual exploration of whatever content is under consideration. The teacher seeks to encourage students to explore possible initial meanings of the story (or other stimulus) and then 'bridge' that discussion to explore the meaning of the philosophical concepts underpinning the story, such as the nature of 'truth' and 'beauty'. Whatever stimulus is used, it should be contestable, that is, have sufficient ambiguity to resist attempts to define it with complete finality. Better still if the stimulus is controversial.

Whether these programs can still be called Philosophy for Children is a matter for debate. However, all these programs remain based on and heavily influenced by Lipman's Philosophy for Children. Consequently, the term 'Philosophical Inquiry' will be used interchangeably with 'Philosophy for Children' in this text, given the caveats.

So, this book, consistent with Lipman's original aims, is about helping children become more thoughtful, more reflective, more considerate and more reasonable[1] (p. 15). The integration of critical thinking into every aspect of the curriculum sharpens children's capacity to make conceptual connections and distinctions. Practicing collaborative inquiry has implications for improving student learning and helps students express themselves better. Academic performance can be no better than the thinking skills that underlie that performance.

Teachers 'Making a Difference' Through Philosophical Inquiry

This section considers philosophical inquiry from a teacher perspective. Teaching is essentially an interpersonal activity. As Christopher Day[9] quoted in his introduction to *A Passion for Teaching*: 'Teachers are the human point of contact with students. All other influences on the quality of education are mediated by who the teacher is and what the teacher does. Teachers have the potential for enhancing the quality of education by bringing life to the curriculum and inspiring the students to curiosity and self-learning.' (p. 3).

Teachers matter. Teachers have been estimated to have two to three times the impact of any other school factor[10]. A synthesis[11] of over 500,000 studies found sixteen of the top twenty influences on student achievement to be under the control of the teacher. Interestingly, the second most powerful effect on student achievement ('students' prior cognitive ability'), was described as something that teachers cannot influence. However, *A Teacher's Guide to Philosophy for Children* will argue that regular participation in Philosophical Inquiry *can* influence cognitive ability. The observation that teachers 'make a difference' raises the question as to how teachers can best be supported to make that difference. Encouraging collaborative inquiry is seen as one way of expanding the teacher's 'toolbox'. The approach also helps 'future proof' youngsters. They are better able to cope with change and the rate of change, and using the four Cs (critical, creative, collaborative and caring thinking) can build on and make use of change.

However, teachers are not free agents and their teaching is influenced by factors at different levels[12]. These include government directives prescribing how the curriculum should be 'delivered'. If the curriculum becomes narrowed to tight measurable objectives, such directives can put pressure on the teacher to 'teach to the test'. Tight objectives also tend to influence classroom dynamics, reinforcing traditional teacher-student communication patterns. Such patterns (discussed in Chapter 7) can test recall but contrast with teachers' improving logical thinking and understanding through regular participation in collaborative inquiry (discussed in Chapters 5 and 6). Inquiry underpins good teaching practice. While recitation restricts discussion, inquiry encourages students to engage, allowing issues to be freely explored. Philosophical inquiry is about nurturing curiosity and provides a way forward. The current book offers a process and possibilities that can be practiced despite a background climate working against space for thinking.

The needs of students are inseparable from the needs of those educating them. *A Teacher's Guide to Philosophy for Children* maintains that philosophical inquiry provides an enriching experience for both educators and students. Teaching is seen in this context as a moral enterprise that exceeds any mechanistic 'transmission' of the curriculum. The two Latin roots of the word 'education' (*educare* – to train and *educere* – to draw out) are both reflected in this process. As advocated by Socrates, philosophical inquiry encourages students to become better at asking questions and not just be masters of answering questions. Haynes[13] found teachers described a sense of liberation derived from the spontaneity of inquiries. 'They describe some initial fear of the open space of unscripted teaching, followed by a sense of release and excitement as they learn the role of philosophical facilitator, listening to children's thinking and responding in the moment.'

In the United States, it has been reported[14] that 'Teacher morale, according to various surveys, has plummeted in recent years, with educators saying that school reform has made them the scapegoat for problems in public education.' In England such concerns have been similarly reflected[15]. While increased workloads have reduced teacher satisfaction[16], it is also likely that a results-driven environment has made it more difficult to set aside time for students being able to think together to explore issues in more depth. While Philosophical Inquiry is not going to provide a panacea to these concerns, it has a place in providing an occasional and effective classroom antidote to more rigid practice.

Philosophical Inquiry: Both 'Practical' and 'Evidence Based'

A Teacher's Guide to Philosophy for Children is evidence based and seeks to bridge the gap between research and practice. Unfortunately, research evidence often fails to get translated into classroom practice. In recent years teachers have often felt overwhelmed by relentless waves of government initiatives. This trend has not been evaluated in terms of what is 'most effective'. For example, it has been suggested[17] that 'Teachers have little regard for the findings of educational research, seeing it as having limited, if any, practical value' (p. 4). It has also been suggested[18] that many existing school practices are inconsistent with what is known about effective learning and that the influence of research on professional practice has been weak. A proposal[19] that educational psychologists should translate research evidence into more user-friendly forms for teachers so that it can be applied to real world classroom contexts is reflected in this book.

A Teacher's Guide to Philosophy for Children is particularly relevant to translating research evidence about classroom dialogue into practice. In this context, Murphy[20] recognized that 'successful implementation in classrooms requires buy-in from a host of educational stakeholders, including district administrators, building principals, teachers, students and care-givers'. Murphy cautioned that 'buy-in' is not easily obtained. However, successful buy-in was exemplified by the authors' Thinking Through Philosophy project in a whole local authority (school district) that optimized a context where teachers regularly inquired with their students.

A Psychological and Educational Perspective on a Philosophical Process

A key aim of this book is to develop student habits of thinking critically. Both psychology and philosophy are concerned with critical thinking. Philosophers have been developing rigorous ways of thinking about logic and the nature of knowledge for millennia. Philosophy can be also regarded as a structured search for truth using reason and good argument. Psychologists have had a more recent history, but have developed a range of empirical scientific methods to test theories and build practical models of how humans develop their thinking. Unusually for a book on Philosophical Inquiry, the authors have approached this subject from a psychological perspective. Together, psychological and philosophical perspectives powerfully inform educational practice to promote learners who are able to critically analyze and apply what they are learning beyond the classroom.

Apart from the practical educational benefits of Philosophy for Children, encouraging children and young people to voice their views is consistent with the United Nations Convention on the Rights of the Child[21]. This Convention is the most widely ratified human rights treaty in history and gives children the legal right to express views freely and to freedom of expression and thought. Although the United States government played an active role in the drafting of the Convention, the United States is the only country other than Somalia that has not ratified the Convention[22]. So, while there is not any binding legal obligation under international law, it seems particularly apposite for American schools to support the spirit of the Convention through a process that gives children a voice as part of their educational experience and development. *A Teacher's Guide to Philosophy for Children* helps teachers to achieve this.

The Structure of This Book

The current chapter introduces Philosophy for Children and sets the scene for the rest of the book by summarizing the main ideas in each of the subsequent chapters. This first chapter also starts to explore philosophical inquiry as a fulfilling addition to the teacher's repertoire of skills. While the book explores developing the *practice* of inquiry in classrooms, the need to base such practice on sound research evidence is also emphasized. Recognition is given to the need for research findings to be expressed in simple terms for practitioners who do not have the luxury of time to pore over the details (and sometimes obtuse language) of research reports.

Chapter 2 discusses the aims of Philosophy for Children and explores some key issues relating to both teachers and students. The chapter considers what makes a question philosophical and whether the inquiry has to be philosophical in the first place. Consideration is given in this and other chapters as to how a teacher can make time for philosophical inquiry in the context of competing demands and a crowded curriculum.

The characteristics that make facilitators well placed to help children contribute to inquiries are discussed. The chapter also considers the extent to which younger inquirers are capable of abstract reasoning and philosophical thinking.

Chapters 3 and 4 are both highly practical chapters. The key elements of the Thinking Through Philosophy (TTP) approach are described in Chapter 3. It looks at the details of each element and how they might be combined to form a cohesive approach in the classroom. Information on useful types of questioning is given to show how to 'dig deeper' into a philosophical question. Alongside are practical strategies showing how to build a richer inquiry. Templates are provided (and are also available on an accompanying *Resources Website* so they can be printed off), along with guidance in how to complete them in order to build an Inquiry Plan. There is a range of games and activities that can used to develop and reinforce skills useful to facilitating an enquiry. Details of some of these are given in order to show their place in the method and how they may be used in a classroom. The idea that inquiries within a particular community (classroom) may mature and develop over time is introduced, related to three stages of the development of an inquiry and information. There is a detailed description of the three stages and information on how and when to move from one to the other.

Chapter 4 describes the Thinking Through Philosophy project, how it came to be undertaken and how it spread across a whole school district. It shows some of the reasons for particular elements being included in the approach and gives a description of the support given to teachers in the project. Examples are given of different approaches to introducing philosophical inquiry – for example, a whole school approach, a 'Beacon School' approach where one school is the lead organization for the area, a small 'cluster' approach and a whole school district approach. Evidence from Hungary, Grenada and India is included to connect with this last point, showing effectiveness in hugely different educational, social and cultural contexts. The chapter describes potential classroom difficulties and strategies for success, and also gives anecdotal evidence of what classroom teachers found successful and important when first introducing philosophical inquiry. This chapter reinforces the idea that the method can be successful in a wide range of educational or social contexts.

Chapter 5 explores in more detail how P4C can help students become more independent thinkers and learners. Thinking and learning are closely intertwined. P4C has implications for students becoming more effective learners as they construct more meaningful understandings. P4C encourages students to consider evidence supporting (or negating) their particular beliefs and viewpoints. The influence of beliefs (attributions) about our abilities in learning is also considered. We know that students who are able to reflect on their learning and thinking processes (i.e., have metacognitive strategies) are more effective learners than those who do not. We look at how regular practice in philosophical inquiry encourages metacognitive reflection on thinking and learning. We also draw connections between the practice of P4C and what we know about the psychology of cognitive development.

Chapter 6 will explore what higher or more complex thinking skills are, why they matter in contemporary society and how P4C can promote such skills. Particular emphasis is given in this chapter to *critical* thinking, including what we mean by critical thinking and a discussion of the sub-skills that contribute to critical thinking.

Chapter 7 considers how P4C meets the emotional needs of learners and promotes their social development. The strong connection between thinking and feeling is explored. Consideration is given to the contribution of inquiry to student's emotional health and why this is the case. The chapter places P4C in the wider context of how classroom talk in general can be used to strengthen communication and participation.

Chapter 8 will be of interest to those who seek evidence of outcomes from P4C. It is important that in an era of ever-changing educational fashions and fads, practitioners are confident that philosophical inquiry has a sound evidential base. Although far from a simple panacea, P4C has proven durable since Lipman's first publications in the early 1970s. This chapter includes the authors' findings from an evaluative four-year longitudinal study, together with a wider summary of other evaluation findings relating to P4C. We live in an era when concerns are regularly expressed about the validity of information. In 2016 the Oxford Dictionaries declared 'post-truth' to be their international word of the year[23]. Defined by the dictionary as an adjective 'relating to or denoting circumstances in which objective facts are less influential in shaping public opinion than appeals to emotion and personal belief', dictionary editors said that use of the term 'post-truth' had increased by around 2,000% in 2016 compared to the previous year.

Chapter 9 is of practical benefit to those who facilitate inquiries, by giving them some tools to help them evaluate whether those inquiries have worked. A range of measures are identified, from objective, quantitative ones to subjective, qualitative ones. Of course, different measures take up different amounts of time, which is a consideration. How can you use data you would have been gathering anyway for the wider purposes of evaluating your inquiries? And how can you find time to analyze your data and report it, first to other teachers in the school then maybe to wider interest groups?

Chapter 10 considers how the community of inquiry can be taken as a microcosm for participation in broader democratic institutions. In a time when there are concerns about fake news distorting and undermining democratic discourse, this chapter looks at how P4C can inoculate students from being easily manipulated by emotive views that lack any rational basis. P4C encourages questioning and inquiring minds, so students critically evaluate information they are exposed to.

The concluding Chapter 11 considers how inquiries can be sustained and embedded in educational practice. Sustaining philosophical inquiry in the classroom is far from straightforward in educational contexts riven with competing demands and pressures. Many innovations in education (even when evidence based) come and go as teachers and their enthusiasms change. Sustainability issues are considered at the level of the individual teacher, the whole school district and national education systems. Lessons (including some painful ones) learned in sustaining inquiry in schools will be shared.

References

1. M. Lipman, A. M. Sharp and F. Oscanyon, *Philosophy in the classroom*. 1980. Philadelphia, PA: Temple University Press.
2. *Society for the Advancement of Philosophical Enquiry and Reflection in Education (SAPERE)*. Available at: www.sapere.org.uk/Default.aspx?tabid=162 [November 27, 2018].
3. M. Gregory. Precollege philosophy education: What can it be? The IAPC Model. In S. Goering, N. J. Shudak and T.E. Wartenberg (Eds.). *Philosophy in schools: An introduction for philosophers and teachers*. 2013, pp. 69–85. New York: Routledge.
4. C. C. McCall. *Transforming thinking: Philosophical inquiry in the primary and secondary classroom*. 2009. London: Routledge.

5. R. Sutcliffe. Evolution of philosophy for children in the UK. In Anderson, B. (Ed.) *Philosophy for children: Theories and praxis.* 2017, pp. 3–13. Abingdon: Routledge.
6. R. Fisher. *Stories for thinking.* 1996. Oxford: Nash Pollock Publishing.
7. P. Cam. *Thinking together.* 1998. Alexandria, NSW: Hale & Iremonger.
8. P. Cleghorn. *Thinking through philosophy.* 2002. Blackburn, England: Educational Printing Services.
9. C. Day. *A passion for teaching.* 2004. London: RoutledgeFalmer.
10. RAND Corporation. *Teachers matter: Understanding teachers' impact on student achievement.* 2012. RAND Corporate Publications Document Number: CP-693/1 (09/12).
11. J. Hattie. *Visible learning.* 2008. London & New York: Routledge.
12. U. Bronfenbrenner. *The ecology of human development—Experiments by nature and design.* 1981. Cambridge, MA: Harvard University Press.
13. J. Haynes. Freedom and the urge to think in philosophy with children. *Gifted Education International,* 2007, vol. 22, pp. 229–237.
14. L. Sutcher, L. Darling-Hammond and D. Carver-Thomas. *A coming crisis in teaching? Teacher supply, demand, and shortages in the U.S.* 2016. Washington, DC: Learning Policy Institute.
15. House of Commons Education Committee. *Recruitment and retention of teachers.* 2017. London: Her Majesty's Government.
16. D. Hughes and G. Hitchcock. *Research and the teacher: A qualitative introduction to school-based research.* 1995. London: Routledge.
17. M. S. Donovan, J. D. Bransford and J. W. Pellegrino (Eds.). *How people learn: Bridging research and practice.* 1999. Washington DC: National Academies Press.
18. C. Day et al. *Teachers matter: Connecting work, lives and effectiveness.* 2007. London: Open University Press.
19. R. H. Shute. Promoting mental health through schools: Is this field of development an evidence-based practice? *The Psychologist,* 2012, vol. 25, issue 10, pp. 752–755.
20. P. K. Murphy et al. What really works: Optimising classroom discussions to promote comprehension and critical-analytic thinking. *Policy Insights from the Behavioral and Brain Sciences.* 2016, vol. 3, issue 1, pp. 27–35.
21. United Nations General Assembly. *Convention on the rights of the child.* 1989. New York: UNGA.

22. Human Rights Watch. *United States ratification of international human rights treaties*. 2009. Available at: www.hrw.org/ news/2009/07/24/united-states-ratification-international-human-rights-treaties [September 1, 2018].

23. 'Post-truth' declared word of the year by Oxford Dictionaries. *BBC*. November 16, 2016. Available at: www.bbc.com/news/ uk-37995600 [November 27, 2018].

2

Aims and Process of Philosophy for Children

John Dewey famously said in his book *Democracy and Education* in 1916: 'Education is not an affair of "telling" and being told, but an active and constructive process'[1] (p. 19). So, what *is* Philosophy for Children? It provides a method that enables 'students to construct their own understanding rather than having teacher knowledge told to them. This chapter will set the scene for the next two chapters where practicalities are considered in more detail.

Philosophical inquiry is about making meaning (or sense) of concepts and putting meanings to the test of truth. It can be regarded a structured search for truth in important questions using reason and good argument. Philosophy for Children is concerned with the development of a community of inquiry, a community where students think together and build on each other's ideas. The process of inquiry can be applied to any subject and almost all inquiry can be described as philosophical in nature. Philosophy is essentially a process of asking questions and thinking about answers to those questions. Very often there is no answer to a philosophical question and it will throw up more questions. However, through the process of inquiry there should be forward movement so that by the end more is known about the question. The participants move further toward an answer even if it is not considered as a final absolute answer. Even in science answers/truths are now held as 'holding positions'. It is good to encourage the results of philosophical inquiries to be considered in the same light.

Philosophy for Children is the activity that children engage in when discussing philosophical questions. Students and their teacher share a short story, picture, poem, object or some other thinking stimulus. In a mature community the children then take time to think of their own questions before one is selected for more extensive discussion. The teacher reinforces a climate that encourages participation. Ground rules are set in advance that encourage showing respect for everyone. Students construct their own conceptions of whatever topic is being considered. If someone disagrees, they must find a good reason to express that disagreement (as against simply saying that the other person is 'wrong'). Philosophical inquiry is not a 'tool-kit' approach to promoting independent thinking and the process is dependent on the quality of interaction and dialogue engendered rather than assiduously following a simple step-by-step procedure[2].

Philosophy for Children tends to focus on concepts that are intrinsically interesting to children, such as fairness, justice, friendship, rights, love, identity, knowledge, truth and free will. It draws on practical Socratic discussion as against more academic philosophizing. The teacher helps the students build constructive dialogue in which concepts are clarified, meanings explored and a shared understanding is achieved. In Philosophy for Children, the slow thinker with a sound argument is no less respected than the child who presents their views quickly and articulately[3] (p. 43). It is about giving young students the opportunity to express ideas confidently in a safe environment.

Philosophical inquiry seeks to gradually build classroom dialogue and requires students to listen carefully to each other's views. The quality of the dialogue is helped by the simultaneous development of the language of inquiry, initially by the use of protocols and imitation. Dialogue differs from debating in that the emphasis is more on reflective learning than on 'winning' an argument. Dialogue also differs from conversation in that conversation implies the stating of personal opinions without justification or reason. Dialogue, by contrast, is an exploration of ideas – an inquiry. So, philosophical inquiry is about exploring great ideas, asking open questions and participating in engaging activities that generate a better understanding of a concept.

What Makes an Inquiry Philosophical?

Teaching philosophy to children throws up many questions, such as 'What is a philosophical question?', 'Can children do philosophy?' and 'Do teachers need a philosophical background to lead inquiries?' *A Teacher's Guide to Philosophy for Children* will define the term 'philosophical' in a broad and practical sense. Philosophy for Children moves away from direct instruction of targeted knowledge to more spontaneous (and satisfying) exchanges that freely explore ideas. While the teacher gives up some control of the *content* of student contributions, the *process* remains under the control of the teacher. A method and rules are necessary to prevent a conversational free-for-all.

A Teacher's Guide to Philosophy for Children considers philosophy to be thinking deeply about complex philosophical questions. This involves developing the capacity to pose questions and respond to others in a thoughtful rational way. It is also about a search for truth and meaning in important questions using reason and good argument. The word 'Philosophy' could bring to mind an abstract approach not well fitted to the harsh demands of real contemporary education. However, Philosophy can and should be about exploring concepts that directly relate to the student's world and therefore are of relevance and interest to them. For example, having a dialogue about bullying could be helpful not only with regard to reducing bullying but also to developing thinking more generally.

When students are encouraged to question and develop their own opinions, they can be said to be philosophizing. A philosophical question invites people to pool and resolve their differing viewpoints in response to an open question. Children (and adults) are much more open to changing their mind (therefore showing reasonableness) by considering other points of view and the evidence that accompanies them. 'Big' open-ended philosophical questions inquire into moral, ethical and spiritual questions and invite reflection on values, beliefs and meanings. These questions lack simple answers. Many problems facing not only individuals but also nations lack simple answers. Despite this, politicians sometimes seem compelled to come up with simple solutions to complex issues in adversarial climates that fail to recognize the validity of other viewpoints.

What Are the Aims of Philosophy for Children?

Teachers are likely to be motivated to invest their time and energy in Philosophy for Children if they believe the thinking, learning and social development of their students will show tangible benefit from engaging in inquiries. Philosophical inquiry develops the ability to express oneself and provides a method that can be used in all school subjects. It provides practice in listening, keeping to the point, assessing assertions and substantiating one's own point of view.

1. Developing Independent Thinkers

The overall aim of Philosophy for Children is 'to help children learn how to think for themselves' and make informed choices[3] (p. 53). The goal of the program is to improve children's reasoning abilities and judgment by having them think about thinking as they discuss concepts of importance to them. An independent thinker is able to organize their thinking through questioning, hypothesizing and suggesting alternative explanations. Their conclusions are directly linked to their reasoning from evidence. The UNESCO Philosophy report[4] states that Lipman's primary goal was to foster critical thinking and formal logic in particular. Lipman believed that children have the ability to think abstractly and understand philosophical questions from an early age. While the scientific method can contribute to critical reasoning, the skills of philosophy address more abstract questions, for example, 'Do we have free will?', 'Is there a God?' and 'What is greed?'. The ambiguity of such questions maximizes the scope for eliciting different views and justifying one's argument rationally.

Lipman suggested that Philosophy for Children encourages children to develop critical and creative thinking skills through collaborative dialogue. Reasoning skills are central to critical thinking and involve students justifying their views with reasons, drawing inferences, making deductions, identifying underlying assumptions and dealing with contradictions. Ill-defined concepts are clarified, sweeping generalizations avoided and decisions informed by reasons and/or evidence. The facilitator encourages reasoning through probing questions to help student's judgments become more balanced. Examples of such questions would be 'How do you know that?', 'Can you explain what you mean by saying something is not fair?' and 'Can you give me an example of what you are saying?' Reasoning is sharpened and perfected by disciplined discussion[5] that leads to better judgment and open-mindedness. Disciplined discussion calls for reasons, not interrupting, celebrating changes of mind and the general disposition to think better.

Students develop inquiry skills through Philosophy for Children. Examples and counterexamples are encouraged during inquiries, and evidence is routinely requested to support views expressed by others. Subtleties in the meaning of words are explored through making distinctions between similar concepts and identifying connections between concepts. Careful listening is necessary to understand and be sensitive to the thoughts and feelings of the speaker.

Lipman's original model aimed to cultivate 'creative thinking' as well as 'critical thinking'. Creative thinking skills are reflected in generating ideas and hypotheses and are encouraged by questions such as 'Can we suggest another question?' or 'Is there another possible interpretation of this?' In practice, critical and creative thinking are seen as interdependent, that is, effective critical thinking always involves an element of creativity, and to be effective creative thinking necessitates some critical appraisal of possibilities.

Lipman later extended his critical and creative thinking model to one that including caring and collaborative thinking. These have been referred to as the 'four Cs'. Students are encouraged to think caringly as they participate in their communities of inquiry. They are encouraged to think ethically and to have a concern for those who take part in the inquiry as well as caring for the quality of the dialogue. Caring is reflected in ground rules such as 'We listen attentively to each other'. Caring thinking builds a sense of community when proper respect is paid to differences in interpretations, beliefs and views. Without such care it is unlikely that the outcome of the dialogue will be determined solely by the better reasoned argument.

The fourth 'C' in the framework is 'collaborative thinking'. Collaborative thinking makes explicit the need to genuinely respond to and build on other's ideas and to support them to articulate thinking. Collaborative thinking is reflected in notions such as 'we share ideas', 'we build on each other's ideas' and 'we try to understand other points of view'.

So, the best inquiry outcomes require a balance between the four C's. Caring and collaborative thinking avoids 'disputational talk'[6] characterized by a lot of disagreement and a competitive atmosphere. Similarly, the absence of critical and creative thought will leave us with unreflective 'cumulative talk', which is described as everyone simply accepting and agreeing with what other people say without any critical evaluation. When encouraging children to think critically, caringly, creatively and collaboratively, Lipman suggested that we need to make reasoning more emotional and emotions more rational. Philosophical inquiry encourages decisions that balance the rational and the emotional, thereby being more 'reasonable'.

2. Developing More Effective Learners

Teachers are likely to be far more interested in facilitating inquiries if they have relevance to learning. Philosophy teaches students a range of skills necessary for academic success – careful listening and analysis, assessing the validity of what is being heard and developing an argument in support of a position. When students construct personal understandings, they are more likely to be able to connect their learning to what they have previously learned. Deeper processing and thoughtful reflection make it more likely that learning can be applied to the real world (in marked contrast to rote learning).

When students are able to analyze what they are learning and make more logical inferences, they draw better conclusions and achieve better learning outcomes. Philosophy for Children encourages students to make more reasoned arguments to support their point of view. This applies to students of all ages although the degree of sophistication of their argument will vary with the maturity and cognitive level of the student. Encouraging students to be more reflective and aware of how they think and learn (i.e., to become more metacognitive) enables them to take increased responsibility to effectively manage their learning.

Research evidence[7,8] indicates improvements in students' cognitive ability following regular weekly participation in philosophical inquiry. Importantly, cognitive reasoning ability is correlated with learning outcomes[9]. Sound reasoning is relevant across the curriculum. Practice in inquiry in the longer term is thus likely to support learning outcomes.

3. Promoting Social and Emotional Development

The experience of having one's ideas carefully listened to is likely to strengthen self-esteem and confidence. Children learn to avoid dismissing different views without examining them properly. They learn that they can disagree without falling out. Lipman's vision for the classroom was that of a community in which friendship and cooperation were welcomed as positive contributions to a learning atmosphere, rather than the semi-adversarial and competitive conditions that prevail in too many classrooms. The process of shared inquiry appears to help meet student's key emotional needs for competence, autonomy and relatedness. The relevance of these psychological needs has been highlighted by Deci and Ryan[10] and will be elaborated in Chapter 7.

Philosophy for Children also engages with the notion of emotional intelligence[11]. The process of philosophical inquiry can be used as a tool to explore the emotional realm, which builds competence and autonomy and also emotional quotient (EQ). It is therefore a by-product of the process as well as a 'targeted' area.

4. Developing Students' Ability to Participate
   in and Support Democracy

Healthy democracies require citizens who can take part in rational discussions and communicate their views coherently. Lipman argued that stimulating critical thinking in children in a community of inquiry is a means of educating them for democracy. P4C has sometimes been taken up as much for its potential in developing participatory democracy and healthy citizenship as for its potential for cognitive enhancement or social development. In order to fully participate in a democracy, we need to be disposed to listen, to tolerate different viewpoints and to have an attitude which says that all answers are good until the opposite is proved. Effective participation also requires weighing evidence, being aware of reasons for one's beliefs and understanding why others may have a different view. A healthy democracy thus depends on its citizens feeling they can participate in and shape their community for the benefit of all.

What Skills, Attitudes and Knowledge Do Teachers Need to Facilitate Inquiries?

A *Teacher's Guide to Philosophy for Children* contends that teachers do not need to be familiar with philosophical literature in order to facilitate philosophical inquiry. What is more important is an attitude of genuine (philosophical) curiosity, open-mindedness and an ability to inquire *with* students. Teachers need to be comfortable communicating that they may not have a definitive answer themselves to the issues under consideration. What the teacher has is control over the process that allows students to pursue the inquiry.

Teachers familiar with Piaget's stages of cognitive development could dismiss the exploration of philosophical concepts as too abstract to be usefully discussed by young children. Similarly, it has sometimes been argued that philosophy is more useful for 'intellectually gifted' children[12]. Such students are seen as preferring more conceptually demanding activities over those they judge to be too easy or repetitive. However, others[13,14,15] have argued that children as young as five or six years of age can be encouraged to think for themselves and make choices and judgments that require justification, albeit at a simpler level. Stanley[16] provided an account of using P4C with five-year-olds to build skills of justifying choices, making connections and discovering themes and concepts. For example, children might be encouraged to discuss what makes 'good' characters good and 'bad' characters bad.

The observations of the authors in the Thinking Through Philosophy project were that students from six to sixteen years and of different abilities can benefit from participating in inquiries. This is entirely consistent with the age range targeted in Lipman's original Philosophy for Children program. The present authors are familiar with teachers' reports of outstanding (secondary school) students who did not initially perform well in P4C because they were not used to thinking for themselves, justifying ideas, etc. They had learned to do well in the 'absorb and regurgitate' scenario.

During P4C the teacher models curiosity during the inquiry process and encourages students to engage by seeking their views, reasons and questions. The skills of the teacher in developing a supportive emotional climate are crucial as emotional security needs to be cultivated to enable members of the group to contribute. Teachers communicate a genuine interest in and respect for what students are saying through pursuing student comments no matter how trivial these may appear at first. Interaction sequences between teacher and students conducive to inquiry will be analyzed in more detail in Chapter 7. Students are challenged to think for themselves through gentle but rigorous open-ended questioning. The facilitator may also reflect back discussion in the form of summaries or restatements, such as 'So you think that…?' or 'Is this what you were saying?'

Lipman suggested important conditions for teaching P4C. He argued that teachers need to consistently model an endless 'quest' for meaning and truth. In doing this, teachers should avoid implanting their own views and values to give students the space to construct their own. The teacher needs to disguise their own personal viewpoint on an issue. Many younger students want to agree with the teacher whatever their viewpoint. (And maybe older ones want to disagree!) Children need to develop the capacity to judge for themselves. It is about the way children should think, not what children should think. Respecting children's opinions that are different from the teacher's own will be difficult if the teacher is certain they already know all the answers. If trust is to be elicited, students should feel able to risk expressing opinions that differ from those of their teacher.

In addition to the above conditions, Lipman also identified teacher behaviors conducive to thinking. Frequent open-ended questioning is used to probe and clarify what the student is saying. He suggested that teachers avoid any tendency to give students answers as this does not help them become independent and resourceful. The teacher needs to look for opportunities to open up a discussion that explores the meaning of concepts readily used in every day speech. For example, if bullying had been raised, the teacher would guide an inquiry as to what we actually mean by 'bullying', so that the students discover the criteria for this concept themselves. The teacher encourages the view that knowledge is something to be created, rather than 'knowledge is answers'.

The importance of listening has already been commented on. Even if the teacher has the ability to listen, there is a natural tendency to quickly interpret remarks from one's own perspective. By their own silence teachers need to leave open a space for speech so that students can articulate exactly what they mean to say. Respectfully listening to student's opinions not only supports thoughtful conversations but is highly valued by students. Students' most valued teacher behaviors have included the observation that the teacher 'listens to you', 'allows you to have your say' and 'really cares about our opinion'[17]. The students' emphasis on 'soft' interpersonal skills did not undermine their views of the importance of teacher qualities such as having high expectations and challenging them to do better.

Teaching children to philosophize (i.e., think for themselves) involves encouraging students to express their ideas and follow logical trains of thought. The quality of the inquiry will depend on the skill with which the facilitator pushes for depth (e.g., by inviting conceptual distinctions) and for breadth (e.g., by inviting conceptual connections). Facilitating a philosophical discussion requires that the group dynamics be monitored and the emotional climate regulated. The teacher has to be able to see which direction a discussion is taking and plan ahead to ensure that it proceeds successfully. The philosophical direction of discussion needs to be managed. For example, in a discussion of the Ring of Gyges (the story of a ring that conferred invisibility, with consequent implications for whether people behaved justly or not), thinking about the relationship between power and good needs to be drawn out, as it is unlikely to happen spontaneously.

The teacher seeks to gradually build a community of inquiry in which students feel comfortable voicing an opinion in front of others. This takes time. Some strategies to promote this will be discussed in Chapter 3. Once a community of inquiry is more established, students are also encouraged to address each other – not just the facilitator. Again, this can take time. The teacher is an active participant. The teacher helps to focus attention on important points and models good questioning by asking for clarification, reasons and evidence. Concepts are explored and defined and ideas expanded. Students are continually encouraged to respond respectfully to each other. Consistent with Lipman's original exhortations, the teacher aims to direct a reasoned discussion rather than being content with a 'mere conversation'.

Are Children Capable of Philosophical Thinking?

The idea of teaching philosophy to children is controversial and this has been thoroughly explored elsewhere.[18] There are counter-arguments to concerns from both a psychological and a philosophical perspective.

Jean Piaget's[19] theory of cognitive development has been used as an argument to suggest children are not capable of philosophical thinking. Piaget suggested that prior to age 10 or 12 most children are not capable of abstract thought as they had yet to reach the 'formal operational stage' of cognitive development. However, there has been a growing body of psychological research[20,21] suggesting that Piaget's account seriously underestimates children's cognitive abilities. Moreover, practitioners of Philosophy for Children[13,15,18] have routinely noted instances where young children demonstrate their ability to analyze and reflect on abstract concepts such as 'freedom' and 'beauty'. Lipman's original Philosophy for Children stories were used with children of all ages.

Philosophers have expressed differing opinions about the suitability of Philosophy for Children. Some philosophers believe children are spontaneously philosophical because of their continual existential questioning and curiosity[4] (p. 5). For those philosophers, to philosophize is considering a question as if for the first time and to learn to approach that question through reasoning. The collaborative nature of inquiry helps make this approach more effective in the classroom. Inquiring with young children can take advantage of common stories as they are often philosophical in nature. They have the potential for raising questions (such as 'What made the ugly duckling ugly?' and 'What then made the ugly duckling beautiful?') that can lead on to fruitful reasoned discussion.

Other philosophers have argued that philosophy is too abstract for many children, suggesting that philosophy is 'unsuitable for school children though perhaps it could be tackled in the sixth form' (i.e., 16–18 years of age)[22] (p. 38). One underlying argument for this view is that children lack the knowledge necessary for philosophical analysis, that is, one has to have sufficient knowledge in the first place in order to critically evaluate that knowledge. Academic philosophers have suggested[23] that 'of course one is always free to define philosophical thinking in a more liberal manner, for example as any and all sorts of "wondering about the world"', distinguishing this from the systematic thinking in which academic philosophers engage. So, the concerns of academic philosophers seem to be about definitions of what constitutes philosophical thinking. As with any skill, we can enact a skill at different levels. For example[24], an NBA all-star basketball player and a kid shooting hoops are playing at different levels but they are both playing basketball. One would not expect a nine-year old to display the same level of sophisticated reasoning as an academic philosopher. Philip Cam[25], in *20 Thinking Tools*, introduces tools used by philosophers (e.g., formal logic) in a form suitable for children and in a way likely to enrich an inquiry.

Another concern about teaching philosophy to children is about its suitability for children with limited language skills. This concern reflects the view that there is no thought without language and that language is necessary for independent thinking. Supporters of P4C believe thought and language develop in concert. They argue that children's thought processes can be improved by developing their language skills and vice-versa. The current authors would concur with the view that thought and language are inter-related and that both can be developed concurrently through participating in a classroom community of inquiry. The present authors have observed four-year-olds with poor language skills begin to explore the nature of reality. Research findings[26] suggest that children from linguistically and socially disadvantaged backgrounds can benefit the most from Philosophy for Children.

Developing Teachers' Facilitation Skills

Reference has already been made in Chapter 1 to the advantages that teachers bring to the role of facilitator of children's philosophical dialogue[27]. While teachers can learn to lead inquiries through on-the-job training[28], learning to implement dialogue-intensive pedagogies can be challenging[29,30]. Developing open communities of inquiry may require a significant shift in pedagogy for some teachers. The role of the teacher as 'curious facilitator' rather than 'expert instructor' may not come naturally to every teacher.

Evidence of a 'teacher effect' in Philosophy for Children has been found[31] in that the extent of student gains can vary from teacher to teacher. However, there were also indications that the practice of teachers in general can benefit from opportunities to develop their skills in facilitating classroom discussion. Several teachers in the authors' experience reported that they felt more comfortable and competent the second year of using the resource because they had (with the children the first year) thought about the issues a bit more themselves! In most people's lives they get few opportunities for deeper level dialogue.

P4C training could be offered during initial teacher education, or as part of the teacher's continuing professional development, or both. Those supporting teachers to facilitate inquiries need to understand the constraints of the classroom and what outcomes can be realistically expected. Direct experience of actual P4C sessions in the classroom is the most useful training. So much the better if training and support are provided to embed P4C in a whole school. However, a whole-school approach is likely to be the exception rather than the rule. Credibility of the trainers in the eyes of the teachers is seen as crucial.

As the community of inquiry works through the children's questions, it is not a matter of convincing others or winning an argument, but of searching together for answers. The right to express one's opinion is counterbalanced by the duty to develop a rational argument. A teacher's skill lies in cultivating intellectual curiosity. There needs to be a method and rules to avoid the session becoming a free-for-all. In this process, teachers have to 'draw out' the student's point of view and show appreciation of the risk that has been taken by the student. We have already noted that teachers must remain vigilant to prevent any dogmatism from taking root by showing that there are always many possible answers to a philosophical question. Otherwise there is a risk the teacher could bring the children's explorations to an abrupt end (as they may feel they now have 'the' correct answer). Similarly, the teacher must equally avoid the trap that all points of view are equally valid. Such a relativist position negates the need to provide a reasoned defense of one's opinion and would, for example, suggest that all ethical stances are equal.

Does Inquiry Need to Be Philosophical?

The question of whether inquiry needs to be philosophical probably needs to define 'philosophical'. Does it matter whether the experience of inquiry is based in exploring philosophical 'big questions' or can the inquiry process be equally applied in other subjects? Are there particular advantages in exploring classic philosophical questions, such as 'Do we have free will?', 'If a tree falls in a forest and no one is around to hear it does it make a sound?' or 'Why are we here?'

Questions around concepts such as beauty, truth, honesty, reality and so on make a personal connection (relationship between the student and the concept) and this is a stage in the process from concrete to abstract, that is, concrete (stimulus) – personal – abstract. For example, in the dialogue between Socrates and Diotima on the nature of beauty, he recognizes the examples of beauty (form, ideas and music) but is constantly brought back to considering the nature of beauty itself. Also, it could be argued that philosophical questions are more open-ended, uniquely ambiguous and perplexing, and therefore provide exceptionally good points to debate and higher cognitive challenge. Teachers tend to find that their approach to structuring a philosophical inquiry carries over into other lessons[32].

For Lipman, philosophy is inquiry. In this sense, practical philosophy would seem essentially to be a process of asking questions and thinking about answers with an emphasis on 'good argument' or reasoning. Education in general can be considered to be an active and reflective process of students constructing their own understandings and judgments rather than of transmission of knowledge from those who know to those who do not know. Lipman states[33] (p. 19) that 'the reflective paradigm assumes *education to be inquiry.*' So, while classic philosophical questions provide a particularly effective stimulus for thinking, the process of inquiry and reflective thinking can be infused into any subject. In Lipman's definition of philosophy, all collaborative inquiry is philosophy.

There are numerous examples of programs and approaches that have developed reasoning and high-quality critical thinking without any reference to philosophy[34,35]. However, the effective processes described exactly mirror those in Philosophy for Children. Similarly, Mercer's[36] work on 'Thinking Together' does not refer to Philosophy for Children but the process of interthinking nevertheless includes the key features of philosophical inquiry. Put simply, for hard-pressed teachers, the more important question is how to engage students in an effective process of collaborative inquiry. Philosophy for Children provides a process for achieving that end.

Infusing Philosophical Inquiry into Other Subjects

Ways in which the process of Philosophy for Children can be infused across the curriculum to enrich leaning have been well documented[2,37,38,39]. The process of Philosophical Inquiry can be applied to explore concepts in science, English literature, mathematics, religious education, and, in fact, any aspect of the curriculum. For example, in relation to history, Haynes[2] suggests that students 'are expected to examine historical evidence and to weigh up change and its consequences' (p. 127) and that inquiry would be an effective way of achieving that goal. The weighing up of evidence and the relationship between events are seen as more important than memorizing discrete 'facts'. Teaching exclusively through inquiry would probably prove excessively challenging for both teacher and student. The need to balance more direct traditional teaching methods with teaching methods that emphasize interactive discussion is not a new finding and is wholly consistent with previous literature on effective teaching[40,41]. The teacher will be the best judge of where that balance lies as this will depend on the unique circumstances of each classroom.

Even if teachers do not consciously apply inquiry processes to other aspects of the curriculum, it appears that the use of Philosophy for Children in the classroom inevitably influences wider teaching and learning. Teachers have found that their experience of structuring philosophical inquiry influences how they teach other lessons. This observation has also been noted by their students[32].

Space for Philosophy for Children in a Crowded Curriculum

One of the perennial issues confronting teachers who wish to 'inquire' philosophically with students is where to place such activities when the existing curriculum is already crowded. As mentioned in the first chapter, high-stakes testing can deter teachers from creating space for open discussion and thinking through inquiry. While there may be short term retention advantages in 'teaching to the test', if students are going to be able to apply their knowledge to real-world issues outside the classroom, they will need be able to think independently. Philosophy for Children aims to promote these skills. Being able to set aside a philosophy hour on a regular basis has the advantage of providing dedicated time so that the whole class has the opportunity to participate in inquiries.

That was the model used in Huntsville (near Houston), Texas[8], when some classes were given the opportunity to inquire as part of each school day. In the Scottish project[7], local government and education administrators gave permission to 'ring fence' a practical one hour philosophy lesson each week. However, pressures on the high school curriculum led to inquiry in high schools being embedded in selected subjects rather than creating a philosophy hour. While this was the case in the U.S.A. and U.K., it may well be true of other countries. So, infusing the inquiry process into other subjects could be used when teachers lack flexibility to allow specific dedicated time for Philosophical Inquiry. All subjects benefit from the inclusion of in-depth group exploration of key concepts through reasoned (and reasonable) argument.

Another way forwards would be that of 'Philosophy after-school clubs', in which students volunteer to attend a regular group outside their main classroom hours. Such groups are not constrained by the curriculum and thus free to explore open philosophical questions. Groups are likely to be smaller and more conducive to participation and students more motivated having chosen this activity. A disadvantage would be that the opportunity to engage in Philosophical Inquiry would not be open to all, and disadvantaged students might be least likely to volunteer to participate.

So, there is no simple answer to the issue of curricular constraints. Ideally, teachers facilitating inquiries with students will be part of a wider supportive school community valuing curiosity and thinking as an essential component of students' education. Teachers should still be able to see scope for offering the experience of philosophical inquiry to their students even if this takes place at different levels (as in the earlier example[24] of shooting basketball hoops) and in different forms.

What This Chapter Has Been About

Consideration has been given in this chapter to a series of important questions that may confront a teacher interested in developing children's thinking through philosophical inquiry. Potential benefits of inquiry have been explored. Philosophical components of inquiry and students' capabilities to inquire have been examined. Practical aspects of how teachers might include inquiry-based practice in their work with students have been discussed. This will set the scene for further practical considerations of developing Thinking Through Philosophy in the next two chapters.

References

1. J. Dewey. *Democracy and education: An introduction to the philosophy of education.* 1916, p. 19. New York, NY: Macmillan.
2. J. Haynes. *Children as philosophers.* 2002. London: RoutledgeFalmer
3. M. Lipman, A. M. Sharp and F. Oscanyon, *Philosophy in the classroom.* 1980, p. 37. Philadelphia, PA: Temple University Press.
4. UNESCO. *Philosophy: A school of freedom.* 2007. Paris, UNESCO. Available at: http://unesdoc.unesco.org/images/0015/001541/154173e.pdf [September 1, 2018].
5. P. Cam. Dewey, Lipman, and the tradition of reflective education. In: M. Taylor, H. Schreier, and P. Ghiraldelli, (Eds.) *Pragmatism, education, and children: International philosophical perspectives.* 2008, pp. 163–181. Amsterdam: Rodopi.
6. N. Mercer, *Words and minds: How we use language to think together.* 2000. Abingdon: Routledge.

7. K. J. Topping and S. Trickey. Collaborative philosophical enquiry for school children: Cognitive effects at 10–12 years. *British Journal of Educational Psychology,* 2007, issue 77, pp. 271–288.

8. F. Fair et al. Socrates in the schools from Scotland to Texas: Replicating a study on the effects of a Philosophy for Children program. *Journal of Philosophy in Schools,* 2015, vol. 2, issue 1, pp. 18–37

9. I. J. Deary et al., Intelligence and educational achievement. *Intelligence,* 2007, vol. 35, issue 1, pp. 13–21

10. E. L. Deci and R. M. Ryan. Motivation, personality, and development within embedded social contexts: An overview of self-determination theory. In R. M. Ryan (Ed.), *Oxford handbook of human motivation.* 2012, pp. 85–107. Oxford: Oxford University Press.

11. D. Goleman. *Emotional intelligence.* 1995. New York: Bantam.

12. R. Sternberg and K. Bhana. Synthesis of research on the effectiveness of intellectual skills programs: Snake oil remedies or miracle cures? *Educational Leadership,* 1996, vol. 44, issue 2, pp. 60–67.

13. G. Matthews. *Philosophy and the young child.* 1982. Cambridge, MA: Harvard University Press

14. N. Maxwell. Philosophy seminars for five-year olds. *Gifted Education International,* 2007, vol. 2, issue 2/3, pp. 122–127.

15. T. E. Wartenberg. Elementary school philosophy. In S. Goering, N. J. Shudak and T. E. Wartenberg (Eds.) *Philosophy in schools: An introduction for philosophers and teachers.* 2013, pp. 34–42. New York: Routledge.

16. S. Stanley. A skills-based approach to P4C – philosophy: Fairy tales and the foundation stage. *Gifted Education International,* 2007, vol. 22, pp. 172–181.

17. J. MacBeath. *Schools must speak for themselves.* 1999. London: Routledge Falmer

18. K. Murris. Can children do philosophy? *Journal of Philosophy of Education,* 2000, vol. 34, issue 2, pp. 261–279.

19. J. Piaget. *Origins of intelligence in the child.* 1936. London: Routledge & Kegan Paul.

20. M. C. Donaldson. *Children's minds.* 1978. London: Croom Helm.

21. J. W. Astington. *The child's discovery of the mind.* 1993. Cambridge, MA: Harvard University Press.

22. S. Johnson. Teaching thinking skills. *Impact No. 8.* 2001. Northampton, England: Philosophy of Education Society of Great Britain

23. R. Fox. Can children be philosophical? *Teaching Thinking*, 2001, vol. 4, pp. 46–49.
24. R. Israeloff. Preface to S. Goering, N. J. Shudak and T. E. Wartenberg (Eds.). *Philosophy in schools: An introduction for philosophers and teachers*. 2013. New York, NY: Routledge.
25. P. Cam. *20 Thinking tools: Collaborative inquiry in the classroom.* 2006. Sydney: ACER.
26. S. Gorard, N. Siddiqui and B. H. See. Can Philosophy for Children improve primary school attainment? *Journal of Philosophy of Education*, February 2017, vol. 51, issue 1, pp. 5–22.
27. M. Gregory. Precollege philosophy education: What can it be? The IAPC model. In S. Goering, N. J. Shudak and T.E. Wartenberg (Eds.). *Philosophy in schools: An introduction for philosophers and teachers*. 2013, pp. 69–85. New York, NY: Routledge.
28. R. Sutcliffe. Evolution of Philosophy for Children in the UK. In Anderson, B. (Ed.) *Philosophy for Children: Theories and praxis*. 2017, pp. 3–13. Abingdon: Routledge.
29. S. Caughlan et al. English teacher candidates' developing dialogically organized instructional practices. *Research in the Teaching of English*. 2013, vol. 47, issue 3, pp. 212–242.
30. I. A. G. Wilkinson, P. K. Murphy and S. Binici. Dialogue-intensive pedagogies for promoting reading comprehension: What we know, what we need to know. In L. B. Resnick, C. A. Asterhan and S. N. Clarke (Eds.) *Socializing intelligence through academic talk and dialogue*. 2015, pp. 35–48. Washington, DC: American Educational Research Association.
31. K. J. Topping & S. Trickey. Impact of philosophical enquiry on school students' interactive behaviour. *International Journal of Thinking Skills and Creativity*, 2007, vol. 2, issue 2, pp. 73–84.
32. S. Trickey and K. J. Topping. Collaborative philosophical enquiry for school children: Participant evaluation at 11 years .*Thinking: The Journal of Philosophy for Children*, 2007, vol. 18, issue 3, pp. 23–34.
33. M. Lipman. *Thinking in education*. 2003, p.19. Cambridge, England: Cambridge University Press.
34. P. K. Murphy et al. What really works: Optimising classroom discussions to promote comprehension and critical-analytic thinking. *Policy Insights from the Behavioral and Brain Sciences*, 2016, vol. 3, issue 1, pp. 27–35.

35. P. C. Abrami et al., Instructional interventions affecting critical thinking skills and disposition: A stage 1 meta-analysis. *Review of Educational Research*, December 2008, vol. 78, issue 4, pp. 1102–1134.
36. K. Littleton and N. Mercer. *Interthinking: Putting talk to work*. 2013. Oxford, England: Routledge.
37. R. Fisher. *Teaching thinking: Philosophical enquiry in the classroom*. 1998. London: Cassell.
38. S. Trickey. How can students be encouraged to think critically? Infusing inquiry across subject disciplines. *Inquiry*, 2010, vol. 25, issue 3, pp. 14–21.
39. L. Lewis and N. Chandley (Eds.) *Philosophy for Children through the secondary curriculum*. 2012. London: Continuum.
40. K. Hall and A. Harding. *A systematic review of effective literacy teaching in the 4 to 14 age range of mainstream schooling*. 2003. London: EPPI-Centre. Available at: http://eppi.ioe.ac.uk/EPPIWeb/home.aspx?page=/reel/review_groups/TTA/English/English_intro.htm [September 1, 2018].
41. K. J. Topping and N. Ferguson. Effective literacy teaching behaviours. *Journal of Research in Reading*, 2005, vol. 28, issue 2, pp. 125–143.

3

From Theory into Practice

Again, we can turn to John Dewey for inspiration, from an even earlier publication: 'I believe that the only true education comes through the stimulation of the child's powers by the demands of the social situations in which he finds himself.'[1] (p. 3). In this chapter we describe the practice of the Thinking Through Philosophy approach to P4C, and how that creates 'thinking challenges' to stimulate the development of the student. This is the method used by both the Texas[2] and Scottish[3] projects. The chapter describes how to make a start, and then how to develop and deepen a philosophical inquiry. Learn to dip your toe in the water and then build your confidence!

The Need for a Structure

Later chapters describe the results teachers have obtained using the Thinking Through Philosophy (TTP) approach[4]. By using this approach, you and your students will get the same outcomes. To use the analogy of baking a cake – there are ingredients and a method to follow. If the baker changes the ingredients or the method a different result ensues. Similarly, of the dozens of P4C lessons we have observed in many different countries, some bore no resemblance to philosophical inquiry – something else had been created, usually unintentionally.

TTP is effective whatever the social or cultural context. One of the authors has been in a small village several hundred miles in the interior of India and heard (through a translator's whispers) a philosophical inquiry developing beautifully. It was a religious festival and the children had come to school on their holiday because of our visit. They mainly lived in crude huts, most did not have electricity and their parents were subsistence farmers or brick makers – yet here they were, exploring a philosophical question and digging into its meaning. We have also been in leafy middle-class areas where 'advantaged' students struggled to construct anything that could be described as either an inquiry or philosophical. To build a firm beginning and foundation it is more about the method than about a particular language or social context of the students, as will be set out in more detail in Chapter 4.

Sometimes after a training meeting a teacher will say: 'Yes, this looks really good, but it won't work with my students because…. (here, fill in any feature or peculiarity of the students, their homes or even the school or teacher)'. Our usual response is: 'So long as your students are human beings, it will work'. However, it is important to understand that what is first described is the *start* of the process of building a community of inquiry and not the end point. It takes time for a community of inquiry to mature and develop. How fast and far this takes place is a combination of both the teacher's skills and experience and the skills and experience of the student group. Keeping with the same analogy, the master baker uses their experience, knowledge and creativity to consciously alter a recipe or method to create something new – something that may be for a particular purpose, audience or occasion. Similarly, the expert facilitator is confidently creative.

In support of the notion that a starting point is needed from which to develop, one can use the Dreyfus model of rule-governed behavior[5]. When anyone is a beginner in any activity, that person needs more guidance or 'rules' to get started and help them build knowledge and practice. A beginner at skiing needs some guidance to get started. The instructor shows how to form a snow plow, bend the knees and gently move down a small slope. After years of practice, as an expert, one does not stand at the top of a black (difficult) run and say 'Form a snow plow, bend your knees a little and gently push off'. No, the skier comes bombing down using all their accumulated skill and experience to automatically read the snow conditions, the slope and the other skiers. So it is with philosophical inquiry – use the method to build your own personal professional knowledge.

What is Philosophical Inquiry in Practical Terms?

The question 'What is P4C?' was answered in Chapter 2, so now our task is to make that approach practical in the classroom. You have seen that dialogue is at the heart of philosophical enquiry and that this is much more than discussion or conversation. It offers the possibility that one's own ideas and perceptions may change in the process – exciting for some, but anxiety provoking for others. The key to developing good dialogue is the skill of the facilitator in asking open-ended questions and encouraging the students to develop the same. It is the 'digging for depth' in thinking (as expressed through dialogue) that is important. Philosophical inquiry seeks to restore the principle of asking questions (which is in fact absolutely natural) and build on this – and a 'community of inquiry' is born! In this process, children learn about learning, and also about themselves as learners. As Fisher put it 'Philosophy is what happens when thinking becomes self-conscious'[6].

What Is a Community of Inquiry?

A community of inquiry is a group engaged in exploring ideas through philosophical dialogue. In schools the community is usually a class. Philosophical inquiry is sometimes called the Socratic method (after the ancient Greek philosopher Socrates) and uses open-ended questioning (described below under Skillful Questioning) to explore issues and inquire after the truth of a matter. The process of dialogue facilitates deeper engagement between the participants and what is under discussion. Matthew Lipman described it as being similar to sailing a yacht against the wind[7]. The boat has to tack, forming a zig-zag pattern across the wind, but there is still forward movement. Similarly, the strands of dialogue can go this way and that way, but most importantly there is a forward movement in understanding. The group knows more about the issue by the end of the dialogue than they did at the beginning.

In practical terms it is important that the students sit in a position in which they can see each other – and this does depend on the layout of the classroom or teaching space. Some teachers use a circle, but sometimes this is not possible and a semi-circle or horseshoe shape may be useful. Having seen many ingenious ways of solving this problem in different classrooms, age groups and countries, the old saying 'Where there's a will, there's a way' comes to mind. This is an aspect of building a supportive, inclusive atmosphere.

The teacher's role is sometimes called 'facilitator' to help distinguish it from the traditional teacher role of imparting knowledge or facts. Indeed, philosophical inquiry helps move away from that anachronistic approach. The role is a dynamic one – sometimes being a participant, sometimes guiding students to deeper involvement, sometimes ensuring that the agreed rules of dialogue are adhered to. It takes practice and, in the beginning, can be like taking a step into the unknown. This is because in a philosophical inquiry there is not a known end point – the teacher is not the only holder of knowledge and ideas or even perhaps the best ideas! We have been in inquiries with six-year-olds and (as a child gives an observation or makes an analogy in trying to make sense of something) thought, 'Wow, I wish I'd thought of that!'

In the beginning the teacher can help develop the inquiry by:

◆ Focusing attention on important points
◆ Modeling good questioning, for example by asking for clarification, reasons and
◆ evidence
◆ Encouraging appropriate student behaviors, such as how to listen to each other and how to respond to each other
◆ Rewarding positive contributions with praise
◆ Not being content with just conversation
◆ Directing the discussion towards Truth

In Chapter 2 it was suggested that it can be difficult for teachers to disguise or withhold their own opinion on the topic or question in the dialogue, but it is very important to do so, especially when a group is just beginning to practice P4C. This will keep the discussion open and exploratory.

The Rational and Moral Dimensions

As we seek to make P4C more practical, one distinction is that a community of inquiry has a rational part and a moral part. The rational part is about building the technical aspects. How can we ensure that inquiry is taking place, that students are exploring an issue deeply, that development in thinking is happening? It includes such aspects as:

◆ Asking open and inviting questions

◆ Giving evidence and examples

◆ Making comparisons

◆ Summarizing and evaluating

◆ Seeking clarification.

More guidance is given later on how to introduce these aspects, as well as how to build in formative assessment. This allows students themselves to be aware of how their community is growing and play a part in that development.

The moral structure includes the application of emotional intelligence and has been called the 'spirit of inquiry'. It is about how members of the community are going to go about the dialogue in terms of their relationships with each other. Is there respect for other views? This area includes the rules of behavior necessary for group activity, such as one person being allowed to speak at a time. This includes ensuring that pupils:

◆ Focus attention on the speaker

◆ Don't 'put down' others

◆ Are not forced to speak

◆ Respect others' views

◆ Are truthful

◆ Are open minded.

There is a sample lesson showing how to democratically build the community 'rules' in the Making a Start section below.

Skillful Questioning

The ability to use 'good' questions (by teacher or students) is at the heart of philosophical dialogue and therefore at the heart of a community of inquiry. You might ask 'what is meant by "good" questions!' 'Good' questions in this context are questions that are open and help the inquiry process, that help uncover more about the subject of the dialogue and that build knowledge of it. Such questions can be divided into groups, examples of which are shown below. By using questions from different groups and at appropriate times during the dialogue, a richer experience will develop. The dialogue becomes deeper and more meaningful. (Inquiring into the meaning of words and trying to make sense of them are of course the beginnings of inquiry and philosophical inquiry – what a teacher wants to see happening in the classroom).

> *Clarifying*. What reasons do you have for saying that? Can you explain more about that?
>
> *Seeking Evidence*. How do you know that? What is your evidence?
>
> *Exploring Alternative Views*. Is there another point of view? Can you put it another way?
>
> *Probing the Superficial*. Why do you think that? What is the cause of that?
>
> *Scaffolding*. If... then what do you think about...? You said... but what about...?
>
> *Testing Implications*. How can we test that in practice? Is that consistent with what you first said?
>
> *Evaluating*. Can anyone summarize the main points for us? Where has our thinking taken us?

These are a few examples about the use of types of question, but a more complete list can be downloaded from the Resource Website accompanying this book (see Download 1).

Useful Strategies for Building the Inquiry

Most people cannot retain the full list of questions in mind all the time, and in any case one could argue that the list is endless. The use of a list is an aid to building skill as a facilitator – throw away this crutch when you no longer need it! Two further points are worth remembering. The first is that a philosophical dialogue is a dynamic process and there is not time to consult lists to ensure an appropriate spread of question types during an inquiry! However, a list will be useful to reflect later on a dialogue and lead to consciously trying to extend one's repertoire of questions as time goes on. Students can also do this as part of the formative assessment of a session. The second point is that being a good facilitator is not just a mechanical process of asking a certain variety of questions, but this is a good way in which to start.

Here are some useful strategies:

- ◆ *Give 'Thinking Time'.* Rapid fire answers may be appropriate in some curricular areas but complex questions to which there may be no single or right answer need time in order to be considered. With this strategy students give longer answers, volunteer answers more readily and give answers that are more analytical, evaluative and creative.

- ◆ *Second Questioning.* Don't always be satisfied with the first answer from a student. On occasion, ask the same person secondary questions to force the person to think more deeply, or perhaps take a different perspective. Handle this with care, informed by your knowledge of the student.

- ◆ *Scaffold.* Where students are struggling to move forward in their thinking, provide some cues or assistance in order to 'kick start' the dialogue again. Ensure this is not from the position of 'knowing the answer' but from that of beginning a new line of inquiry.

- ◆ *Think/Pair/Share.* This is a very useful strategy and will be shown in the planning templates later. When a stimulus (story, poem, picture) has been introduced, as the first action ask students to quietly *think* (with no discussion) what the stimulus was about and of any questions that may be contained in it. Subsequently, a *pair* activity is to have the students discuss with each other what they were just thinking. This not only starts the process, but gives confidence to those who in the early stages may not have confidence to speak to the whole group. The following *share* aspect is where some pairs can put forward their thinking to the whole group.

- ◆ *Ask All Students.* Over a period of time, consciously ensure that all students participate and are involved in the dialogue. It may take a period of time to achieve this, but it is important for each individual as well as the idea of community and valuing everyone.

- ◆ *Good Listening.* A skillful questioner is a good listener. Through focused listening a person can be more 'in the moment' and able to respond more accurately and appropriately rather than in generalities.

- ◆ *Withhold Judgment.* Try to respond in a non-judgmental way by thanking students for their responses and contributions, and continuing to accept a range of alternative views.

Thinking Development, Emotional Intelligence and Spiritual Intelligence

We all think, but left to ourselves, our thinking can often be biased, distorted, uninformed, egocentric or sociocentric. This paints a dismal picture, but perhaps it was ever thus, as 2500 years ago Socrates said after choosing death rather than exile from Athens or a commitment to silence: 'the unexamined life is not worth living' (as recollected by Plato[8] p. 47). Implicit in this is the idea that the quality of our thinking impacts on our lives, both individually and collectively. For the simplest of examples, take the issue of 'fake news' and the potential impact of unexamined acceptance of all we see and hear in the media.

The move to being more critical thinkers must be systematically cultivated and P4C and the TTP approach do just that. Critical thinking is about making an objective analysis and evaluation of an issue or question in order to form a judgment, or at least an informed 'holding position'. By the latter is meant a position that is an advancement on a former understanding but not assumed to be a final absolute position. Examples may often be related to scientific or philosophical questions or ideas. Socrates sought the advice of a woman called Diotima on the nature of Beauty. After considerable advice he determined to spend the rest of his life trying to know Beauty itself. A common philosophical question in P4C is 'What is Beauty?' but it would be a brave or foolish person who gave a definitive answer. Rather, through the process of dialogue, participants can move forward in their understanding of the nature of Beauty.

The processes involved in critical thinking may be broken down to several thinking 'skills' or dispositions. The list may be extensive, but the main ones are:

- *Information Handling.* Processing skills about analyzing, interpreting and locating
- *Inquiry.* Posing and defining problems, planning, predicting and testing conclusions
- *Reasoning.* Giving reasons for opinions, making deductions and making judgments informed by evidence
- *Creative Thinking.* Generating ideas, being imaginative in thinking and being innovative
- *Evaluation.* Evaluating what is heard or read and developing criteria for making judgments.

One of the strengths of the TTP approach is the emphasis placed on the development of emotional intelligence. This is not something new, but there is greater awareness of the importance of it following books by Daniel Goleman, which explored its influence in society. In *Emotional Intelligence*[9] and *Working with Emotional Intelligence*[10] he quoted studies showing that a young person's life chances are at least as much affected by emotional intelligence (EQ) as they are by IQ, and asks, 'Shouldn't we be teaching these most essential skills for life to every child – now more than ever?'[9] When people explore their own ideas, thoughts and behaviors, the possibility opens up that the causes of habitual behavior may be seen. This is very empowering, because at that point *choice* becomes evident. This has an effect not only on the life of the individual, but ripples out to the community. Good critical thinking is not enough – after all, one needs to be a good thinker to be a good criminal or terrorist. The caring aspect of the four Cs were previously introduced, and this is where the emotional begins to be built into the process, as described in the moral part of the structure.

Emotional intelligence includes such aspects as:

- *Self-Awareness.* Knowing how and what you are feeling and how it impacts on your life; having realistic expectations of your abilities

- ◆ *Self-regulation.* Handling emotions so they facilitate the task in hand; having self-imposed boundaries
- ◆ *Motivation.* Having knowledge of motivating factors and forces; having perseverance
- ◆ *Empathy.* The ability to have knowledge of how others are feeling and to use that knowledge in interacting with them; having a rapport with a wide variety of people
- ◆ *Social Skills.* Being able to read social situations, to use skills to persuade, lead, negotiate and compromise.

Spiritual intelligence (SQ) may be seen as further along the spectrum from emotional intelligence. One definition[11] describes it as: 'the intelligence with which we address and solve problems of meaning and value; the intelligence with which we can place our actions and our lives in a wider, richer, meaning-giving context'. In P4C this can include the exploration of larger issues such as our relationship with other living things and responsibilities that may arise from this.

In P4C the EQ and SQ provide the 'fields' within which critical thinking can take place. Of course, it is important that the subject or questions in the dialogue have salience to the students themselves and the whole process does not become a technical or abstract exercise – thinking in a vacuum! The dialogue helps build critical thinking skills, but the emotional and spiritual development is from the themes from which the philosophical question has been derived. This can involve questions about cooperation, bullying, truth and beauty, to name but a few. TTP is not about students practicing for life, but actually living life. What needs to be considered is not just the relationship between P4C/TTP/Philosophical Inquiry and education, but what *kind* of education is wanted, and why?

The Seven Steps to Philosophical Inquiry: Lesson Plan

There are seven steps in the beginning (see Table 3.1). There is no set time limit or time expectation, but for students from age 8 upwards, an hour is often about the average. Schools usually lack flexibility in time available, and in that case the steps can be fit into two school periods. Here are the details of each element, and the reasons for their inclusion.

Table 3.1 The seven steps in philosophical inquiry

Awareness exercise	Quietening and focusing the mind
Last weeks' dialogue	Refreshing previous ideas & bringing new evidence
The stimulus	Providing the basis for the new dialogue
Pair/group work	Thinking about and sharing first thoughts
Philosophical dialogue	The most important element
Closure	Metacognition – thinking about our thinking
Thought for the week	Encouraging further thinking out of the classroom

The awareness exercise. Long before the current enthusiasm for mindfulness, we were using this simple exercise with both adults and students. It is a simple way to help focus attention and be 'in the present' by connecting with the senses. The chatter in the mind subsides, allowing the opportunity to 'give' full attention. The student becomes mentally, physiologically and emotionally in the best state for thinking and learning. The full description and instructions on how to do this are available to download from the book's Resource Website (see Download 2).

Last week's dialogue/practice. This is a short discussion on the last philosophy meeting and an opportunity for students to give further thoughts on it or practical observations related to it. These emerge from encouraging students to keep thinking about a theme or question and to relate what was under discussion to the real world. Senge[12] says that really deep thinking revolves around the iterative cycle of dialogue and action. For example, thinking on the question 'What is Honesty?' takes place during a dialogue, then during the week there is further individual thought and observation on one's actions, related to what was learned during the dialogue. Perhaps the individual may see there is a difference between his or her thoughts and actions. This leads to further thoughts and questions, and so on around the cycle, always digging deeper into more subtle aspects of the question. So, this part of the process reinforces recent learning and relates the theoretical to the world in which the student lives.

The stimulus. The stimulus is to arouse the interest of the group – there is the expectation that something exciting or worth investigating will emerge. It could be a story, a poem, picture or life incident that introduces a theme from which a philosophical question can be derived. There is often some ambiguity in it, or something on which there is no clear consensus. An example is given below (The Donkey's Shadow) in the sample lesson. Aesop's Fables are a very useful source for stimuli – see the Library of Congress for examples (http://read.gov/aesop/001.html). They have been used from the Renaissance onwards for the education of children.

Pair/group work. Students are placed in pairs (or a three if there are an odd number in the group) and asked to discuss their thinking so far. This is about making sure students understood what was happening in the stimulus, and more importantly it contains the beginnings of the exploration of ideas from the stimulus. It is also an area for building student confidence. Those who may be unlikely to offer ideas and opinions initially may be confident enough to speak to a peer partner or in a small group. An important role of the teacher here is to circulate and encourage, perhaps scaffolding if appropriate.

Philosophical dialogue. This is the most important part of the process. Dialogue stimulates a deeper engagement between students and the subject matter and can take learning to a greater level of understanding. It is imperative that during this time the dialogue moves from the concrete to the abstract – from the starting point of the stimulus to the question that has been derived from it. A group of 12-year-olds was observed having a dialogue where the stimulus had been a Greek myth. At the end of the dialogue the group were still fixated on speculating about the mythical characters contained in the story. They had not moved to a philosophical question derived from the stimulus. In the context of P4C it was futile speculation, as it did not lead anywhere – it hadn't moved from the concrete through the personal to the abstract.

Closure. This is the metacognitive stage of the process (which will be discussed further in Chapter 5). It is something that is often missed out in P4C and in education in general. Usually it should not be long and can be a simple practical activity such as

'Thumb tool' or 'Fist of Five' (especially for younger students), both of which are available in the book's Resource Website (see Download 10). In essence, this is about giving closure to the dialogue and providing ways through which students can give attention to how their thinking progressed during the session and ways to improve it in the future – a formative assessment element.

Thought for the week. It is not useful if students hold the view that thinking is something only done in philosophy class! Many of the most useful scientific discoveries have been in reflective moments away from the laboratory or work space. The 'Thought for the Week' is something that the students themselves can learn to formulate. It reinforces the idea of keeping on thinking about something and of looking for practical evidence to support the thinking. An example where the question had been related to Beauty might be, 'During the week look for things you find beautiful. What makes them beautiful? Does Beauty have an effect on you?'

The Three Stages of Development

Stage 1. Introduction of the elements of an enquiry. The teacher chooses the theme and questions. Social and dialogical skills are introduced. Questions are at story/personal/philosophical levels. The teacher ensures the move is made from the concrete to the abstract.

Stage 2. Continuing to build dialogical skills. Consideration of these skills as formative assessment tools. Introduction of Think/ Pair/Share and Connections and Tensions. Students begin to choose the theme for discussion and pose questions at personal and philosophical levels.

Stage 3. Students choose the theme and formulate questions. Voting procedures are varied. Students beginning to interact more with each other rather than everything going through the teacher. There is use of more complex methods of metacognition (see Chapter 5). Students discuss and write the Thought for the Week.

Making a Start

A useful way to introduce P4C to the class is to have a small inquiry (perhaps 15–20 minutes) asking the question 'What is Philosophy?' This will lessen any fear in the students about starting something new – which may at first appear daunting. It is not necessary to come to a definite answer, but rather to interest the group in starting a new and exciting venture together and consider why they are doing it.

Earlier we mentioned the moral aspect of an inquiry, and this involves students setting 'reasonable' rules or social targets through the use of reason and dialogue. Incorporating both these ideas into one lesson, there is an interactive (in the sense of involving the students) lesson available in the book's Resource Website (see Download 3). It can be adapted as required.

From the above lesson will come a number of behaviors useful in facilitating an inquiry, such as one person speaking at a time and the importance of good listening. When printed onto card these are useful in focusing the class on one or two principles per session, and as formative assessment tools. For example, if 'Good Listening' had been a focus of attention (and the card put up as a reminder during the session), in the metacognitive 'Closure' part of the session students would be invited to say whether the quality of listening had been good - what evidence there was for this opinion and what could be done in future sessions to improve it? As examples, a selection of these targets is available for download from the book's Resource Website in a format ready to laminate (see Download 4).

Working in parallel, and used in similar manner, are dialogical targets. These include giving an example, giving evidence or reasons and challenging weak evidence. These are introduced one at a time (i.e., one per lesson) and are discussed to ensure students know both the concept and what it is in practice, and then are also focused on in the 'Closure' section. There is no exact hierarchy to the skills, but certainly some are more difficult than others, so they have been placed in three groups to correspond with the three levels of inquiry that are detailed below. The teacher must use her or his own discretion in planning the introduction of skills suitable for each class. For ease of use, these can be color-coded green, orange and red (see Resource Website Download 5).

The authors are of the opinion that some kind of dialogue plan is always useful in promoting a rich and challenging inquiry. In the early stages this is likely to be more formal in order to support the emerging skills of both facilitator and students. We are aware that teachers in many countries are under time and curriculum content pressures and 'learning on the job' is often necessary.

Stage 1

Table 3.2 is a template showing how the elements of an inquiry, as described earlier, are related. Blank copies can be found in the book's Resource Website to aid planning (see Download 6). This stage of development may take several months practice.

Taking an Aesop's fable (The Donkey's Shadow, see Table 3.3) as the stimulus, here is how it would look in the template below.

Stage Two

At a later date, after weeks of inquiries and when the first group of dialogical skills have been taught and practiced, the second stage may be introduced. Note that two related additions have been made to the

Table 3.2 Planning template – Philosophical inquiry stage 1

Awareness exercise/activity	An energizer if required The awareness exercise
Last week's thought	Discussion of new evidence and ideas related to last week's dialogue
Discussion plan for dialogue	Thinking questions about the story (concrete) (Two or three questions) Thinking questions about the theme (personal) (Two or three questions) Philosophical questions on the theme (abstract) (Two or three questions. Most of the dialogue should be spent in this last area.)
Closure	Brief summary Remember also to use evaluation techniques to focus students on the quality of their thinking (see the toolbox)
Thought for the week	A short statement to focus attention on practical aspects of the theme

Table 3.3 Sample inquiry – Philosophical inquiry stage 1 – The donkey's shadow

Awareness exercise/ activity	Practice the exercise in focusing attention. Praise those who are obviously connected in the present moment and not day-dreaming.
Last week's thought	Remind students of last week's dialogue and ask who can describe the main points. Recall the 'Thought for the Week' and ask who would like to share evidence of their thinking and actions related to it.
Stimulus – Story, poem, activity	A traveler had a long distance to go so he hired a donkey to carry him and his bags. They set off, the traveler riding the donkey and the donkey's owner walking alongside.
	Along the dusty track they went, through the cool forest and up towards the distant hills. After a time, they emerged from the cover of the forest to the bare hills where there was no shade.
	It was a fine day and as time went by it grew hotter and hotter. The traveler wore a hat but still the sweat trickled down his neck and he longed for a drink. He became so hot and thirsty that soon he couldn't stop thinking about having a drink. Oh, for some lovely cool water.
	'I must rest and have a drink,' he said to the donkey owner, who was well used to walking in hot weather. He dismounted and sat down in the donkey's shadow, which was the only shade there was. The owner of the donkey sat in the sun waiting for the traveler to feel better.
	After a while, the donkey's owner also began to feel too hot in the sun. He saw that the only shadow there was, was the donkey's shadow – and there was only room for one person to sit in that shadow! 'Move over,' he said. 'I own the donkey and therefore his shadow too. I want to use the shadow.'
	'But when I hired the donkey, I also hired his shadow,' said the traveler.
	'No, you did not.' The owner gave him a little push.
	'Oh yes I did! A donkey and his shadow cannot be separated, and since I've paid for the donkey, I've paid for his shadow.' Soon the two men were pushing and shoving each other and then thumping and punching.
	While all this was going on, they didn't notice the donkey wandering away, so that eventually when the men fell exhausted to the ground there was no shadow … and no donkey either.[4]

(Continued)

Table 3.3 Sample inquiry – Philosophical inquiry stage 1 – The donkey's shadow (*Continued*)

Discussion plan: Use Think/Pair/Share for one question in the concrete and personal sections	Concrete / Story [Chosen theme – Sharing] 1. Why did the men begin to quarrel? 2. Who do you agree with – the traveler or the donkey owner? Why? 3. Why did the traveler think he owned the shadow? 4. Is it possible to own a shadow? Why? Why not? Personal experience [of sharing] 5. Do you find it easy to share? How does it feel? 6. What sorts of things do you share? Are there things you don't share? Abstract /Philosophical 7. Why do people share? Reasons? Evidence? 8. Why do people not share? Evidence? 9. What is sharing?
Closure	For a closure activity, ask students which idea has been the most important to them, and why. Allow as many to speak as possible. Remember there is no more dialogue at this point.
Thought for the week	During the week, see whether you share or whether you are greedy. How do you feel at the time? What makes you share or not share?

plan – Think/Pair/Share and Connections and Tensions. The Think/Pair/Share comes after the stimulus. In it the facilitator gives 'thinking time' for students to reflect silently on what themes could be drawn from the stimulus. The teacher puts the class into pairs to share the themes they have thought of and give a reason or explanation for their thinking. After a further time comes the 'share' part where pairs can share with the class. At this point the teacher puts all suggestions on the board. There is no discussion or disagreement at this time, so long as each thought offered has a reason given.

When all the ideas have been put up, the students are asked to look at them and see if they can see any connections between them. Again, they must give a *reason* for the connection. These connections are indicated visually by a colored line being drawn between the linked ideas. When all connections have been exhausted (or a suitable time elapsed) the process is repeated, but with the idea of tensions. Tensions are not necessarily opposites but are ideas that clash. These also must have evidence and are indicated by a different color, and thus a 'thinking map' is built up. These two processes are the beginning of getting students to think about themes and potential philosophical questions that may be drawn from them. This preliminary thinking helps the richness and depth of the ensuing dialogue. To help in understanding this concept, an example of what such a connections/tensions display would look like can be found in the book's Resource Website if required (see Download 7). During these weeks further teaching and practice of the orange level of dialogical skills takes place.

Table 3.4 gives a planning template for Stage 2. This stage may also take months to mature properly. Blank templates of Stage 2 can be found in the book's Resource Website (see Download 8).

Table 3.4 Planning template – Philosophical inquiry stage 2

Awareness exercise/ activity	An energizer or calming exercise
Last week's thought	Discussion of new evidence and ideas related to last week's dialogue, and students' practical examples.
Story, poem, activity	The stimulus. It is useful if this has several potential themes. Check the understanding.
Think/Pair/Share	Use Think/Pair/Share to consider main ideas or themes in stimulus. Evidence for this given from the story. Everything is accepted with evidence. Everything is put up on the white board.
Connections and tensions	Students make connections between main ideas / themes based on their own experience. Make a connections map by drawing connecting lines drawn. Repeat with tensions, in a different color.
Discussion plan dialogue	Initially the theme for dialogue can be chosen by the teacher and later by students through voting. Thinking questions about the theme (personal) Philosophical questions based on theme
Closure	Last words. Have our ideas changed? How? Use evaluation techniques to focus students on the quality of their thinking. Use varied techniques.
Thought for the week	A short statement to focus attention on practical aspects of the theme.

Stage 3

After several weeks of working with Stage 2 and the teacher still deciding the philosophical question, the next stage may be introduced. This is having the students frame personal and philosophical questions from the ideas/themes on the thinking map. This is best done collaboratively with the group. The first task is to choose a theme, and this can be done through a simple voting procedure. As an example, let's assume the theme chosen is Honesty. Three or four personal questions related to honesty and the same number of philosophical questions on honesty are needed. For the first couple of times this can be done as a whole class, with some analysis of the questions as they are offered. For the first set of questions, are they related to the theme and personal experience? If not, how might the question be improved? Should it be discarded? For the second group, is it philosophical? Is it too obvious? Is it worth discussing? What makes it so? Once in place, the dialogue begins, following the agreed questions.

A development from this is to have cooperative groups formulate and agree on questions. Each group should write down several questions for each section and have a discussion among themselves about which is the most interesting and why. They then choose one from each section (personal and philosophical) to offer to the class and the teacher writes all the contributions on the board. The class should be given time to read through the questions and form an idea of which they think is the one they would like to explore through dialogue, and why. As described in the preceding paragraph, if a question is seen not to be personal or philosophical it can be challenged – if all agree with the challenge, it is removed from the list. Voting takes place to choose the questions and the dialogue begins.

The above describes a process which can certainly be time consuming. It is important to remember this is just a learning stage and the formality of it will be dropped as dialogue deepens and skills develop. If the time available is restricted, the lesson can be stopped after the questions have been chosen and the dialogue can be a separate session at a later date.

In the real-time introduction of P4C to a class (as opposed to the time taken to read this book), months have probably passed since its first introduction. Students and facilitator will be becoming quite skilled at taking part in, *and sustaining*, an in-depth dialogue. Many of the skills previously described will now be in evidence. In Stage 3,

Table 3.5 Planning template – Philosophical inquiry stage 3

Focusing exercise	Try to vary this exercise. Perhaps a student leading the group through it, perhaps with a focus on a different sense each week, etc.
Last week's thought	The students should be becoming more skilled at contributing further thinking on the last dialogue and where possible relating it to their own lives.
Stimulus – Story, poem, activity	The range and complexity of stimuli grows. They might include media articles, local events, school events, philosophical stories students bring…
Discussion plan	The questions are more often from the students. They may be formed through the Think/Pair/Share process used previously, or through personal quiet reflection after the stimulus is offered for the class to consider. Once questions are listed, the actual choice for dialogue is through a voting process. This can be varied to add interest and some are described in Download 9.
Metacognition – What have we talked about?	Some more complex methods can be used. This section is very important but should not be time consuming. A number of examples suitable from Stage 1 to 3 are available in Download 10.
Thought for the week	Students should be formulating these. The facilitator takes several offered and students choose one.

things are made more challenging for the students and they play more of a part in creating the inquiry. Table 3.5 shows a planning template. Blank templates of Stage 3 are available in the book's Resource Website (see Download 11).

What About Kindergarten?

In Chapter 2 we asked the question, 'Are children capable of philosophical thinking?' and some readers may be a little dubious as to whether this reaches down as far as kindergarten. For us, the earlier critical thinking is introduced, the better. That way it becomes the default mode rather than something new to be learned at a later age. 'Young people come to the early years setting (kindergarten) with a natural sense of wonder and curiosity and as active and eager learners endeavoring to make sense of the world…'[13]. To better understand a P4C session at this level, here is a description of one that was observed with a group of 4-year-olds. These were children from a poorer socioeconomic background with quite poor language skills.

Calming exercise. The group sat on the floor in a circle, the teacher included. She turned to the child on her right and giving eye contact said 'Hello Ruby, welcome to our philosophy class'. Ruby said 'Thank you', and turned to the child on her right. 'Hello Ben, welcome to our philosophy session'. This carried on around the circle. Social norms were thus also being introduced.

Focusing. The teacher had a cloth bag and in it were some plastic animals. A child was allowed to reach into the bag and feel an animal and try to guess what it was. Elsa said, 'It is a cow'. The teacher asked, 'How do you know it is a cow Elsa?' (Looking for evidence). Elsa answered that she can feel four legs and some horns. She is then asked to take the animal out of the bag and see if she is correct. Other children have a turn. Sometimes the evidence has to be probed further – 'Ben you said it is a horse because you can feel four legs. Other animals also have four legs, so is there anything else that makes it feel like a horse?'

Stimulus. The teacher had found a picture (an advertisement) in a magazine that had something incongruous about it. It showed some houses and shops but a big hand was reaching down between the houses. She had copied the picture A4 (letter) size and there was one between two children. For her own benefit she had a small dialogue plan with a few lead questions. The students were asked what was happening in the picture – they had to make sense of it. Ben said it was a giant's hand reaching down to take the French fries (there was a bicycle and in the basket an adult might recognize some French baguettes, but to the child they were French fries!). Elsa said, 'No, I think it is a toy town and a normal hand because the houses don't look real' – giving a counter view and some evidence. And so, the probing and thinking went on for about 20 minutes, by which time they had moved to the abstract and were discussing what is real and not real and how do you know that! Yes, it was in their own language and vocabulary, but 4-year-olds discussing the nature of reality – is there a bigger philosophical question?

Metacognition. The teacher gently asked about what they had started thinking about and what they had ended up thinking about and praised the fact that examples and evidence had been given.

It may be seen in the above example that the general approach to TTP has been followed, yet creatively molded to suit the age and particular group of children. Nonetheless, whatever is chosen for the stimulus must have a level of ambiguity, something that the children have to explore and of which they have to make sense.

A second approach is to use picture books. The teacher reads a story to the class from a picture book and in the usual way may pause from time to time to ask questions about the story. Of course, the pictures are also shared. The dialogue plan (Stage 1) can be followed. An example of this plan, using the story *Marvin gets Mad*[14] can be found in the book's Resource Website (see Download 12). It explores the theme of 'Anger', but also shows that many themes can be drawn from the story. The use of picture books is not just for kindergarten but also very useful in the early grades.

A third approach is to use materials specifically written for kindergarten such as *Thinking with Ava and Grandpa*[15], which uses stories and pictures with integrated philosophical themes. Different levels of questions leading to full inquiries are provided. Another example is *But Why?*[16], which details practical ideas for classroom use. *Laughing Cats and Thinking Trees: A Thinking Curriculum for Pre-school Education'*[17] also contains dialogue plans for kindergarten children.

Sample Themes

One of the advantages of the facilitator retaining some input into the themes for inquiries (as well as when it is related to a curricular area) is that, like all of us, students work from the known. Their knowledge of the possible range of themes is usually more limited than the teacher's, and given total free rein they often revert to just a few favorite genres. It is good to not only stretch their thinking but also the range of what is thought about. A selection of themes is available in the book's Resource Website (see Download 13).

What Next?

The main aspect for the future development of the community that has grown is to continue to challenge students and allow them to challenge themselves. It is not to do the same thing week after week – we all need more than just 'plain vanilla'. Develop your own 'skills toolbox' that began with the use of social and dialogical targets. For example, introduce simple deductive reasoning. An excellent resource is *20 Thinking Tools* by Phil Cam[18]. For variety and better understanding, skills can be introduced using group sets or floor sets. An example of a floor set using the concept of 'Spectrum of Meaning' can be can be found in the book's Resource Website (see Download 14). Allow students who have the ability to facilitate inquiries. Allow them individually or in pairs to plan a whole inquiry. Above all, be creative – remember the analogy of the master baker!

Route Map for Introducing P4C Through TTP

This is for those for whom P4C is a new venture – both teacher and students. Follow this route to the first lesson! Relevant files can be find in the book's Resource Website.

1. Take the 'What is Philosophy' lesson and develop social targets using Download 3.
2. Make social target cards from the above session or use Download 4.
3. Prepare dialogical targets using Download 5.
4. Take your first philosophical inquiry using The Donkey's Shadow or your own lesson. At the beginning, introduce one social target and one dialogical target that will be practiced that lesson.
5. Later, plan a second session using the template in Download 6. Introduce a new social target but practice the same dialogical target. Good Luck!

References

1. J. Dewey. *My pedagogic creed* (Article 1). 1897. Chicago, IL: University of Chicago.
2. F. Fair et al. Socrates in the schools from Scotland to Texas: Replicating a study on the effects of a Philosophy for Children program. *Journal of Philosophy in Schools*, 2013, vol. 2, issue 1, pp. 18–37.

3. K. J. Topping and S. Trickey. Impact of philosophical enquiry on school students' interactive behaviour. *International Journal of Thinking Skills and Creativity*, 2007, issue 2, pp. 73–84.

4. P. Cleghorn. *Thinking through philosophy* (Vol. 3). 2003. Blackburn: Educational Printing Service.

5. S. E. Dreyfus. The five-stage model of adult skill acquisition. *Bulletin of Science Technology & Society*, 2004, issue 24, pp. 177–192.

6. R. Fisher. *Teaching thinking: Philosophical enquiry in the classroom.* 1998. London: Cassell.

7. M. Lipman, A. M. Sharp and F. Oscanyon, *Philosophy in the classroom.* 1980. p. 21. Philadelphia, PA: Temple University Press.

8. Plato and Xenophon. *The apology of Socrates.* 2019. Cambridge: Cambridge University Press.

9. D. Goleman. *Emotional intelligence: Why it can matter more than IQ.* 1996. London: Bloomsbury Publishing.

10. D. Goleman. *Working with emotional intelligence.* 1999. London: Bloomsbury Publishing.

11. D. Zohar and I. Marshall. *Spiritual intelligence: The ultimate intelligence.* 2001. London: Bloomsbury Publishing.

12. P. M. Senge. *The fifth discipline: The art and practice of the learning organization.* 1990. New York: Doubleday.

13. Scottish Government. *Curriculum for excellence.* 2008. Edinburgh: Scottish Government.

14. J. Theobald. *Marvin gets mad!* 2014. London: Bloomsbury Publishing.

15. P. Cleghorn and V. Reid. *Thinking with Ava and Grandpa.* 2008. Blackburn, England: Educational Printing Service.

16. S. Stanley and S. Bowkett. *But why?: Developing philosophical thinking in the classroom.* 2004. Stafford, England: Network Educational Press.

17. M. Lipman, C. Ogden and J. Matkowski. *Laughing cats and thinking trees: A thinking curriculum for pre-school education.* 2003. Montclair, NJ: Montclair State University.

18. P. Cam. *20 Thinking Tools.* 2006. Camberwell, Australia: ACER Press.

4

From Small to Large: Different Contexts for Philosophical Inquiry

After a five-day training course in India in 2018, Pankaj Vyawahare gave thanks and committed to developing P4C in his area: 'Thank you for your great efforts to inculcate and cultivate the thinking culture amongst us for our better tomorrow'. He noted the important aim of making good thinking part of the default attitude or habit of not only one person, but so many people that it becomes part of the culture of an area or country. Good thinking begins as something useful for today, but through our collective efforts becomes part of a 'better tomorrow'. This chapter describes diverse cultural and national contexts that have successfully established philosophical inquiry and gives some guidance on how to put into practice the method described in Chapter 3. These contexts range from the Caribbean to India and from Hungary to Australia. They suggest a universal applicability of the inquiry process.

Lunch Club/After-School Club

The smallest unit is a group who may come from different classes and who meet out of interest because (in most cases) P4C is not part of the school program or curriculum. Of course, this is a useful way of introducing children to the skills and dispositions of inquiry, but time constraints are often a problem and only a small percentage of students in the school benefit. If you are starting a club, it is important to try to generate as much initial interest as possible. Students are giving up their free time and it does take three or four weeks before the love of the inquiry itself generates enthusiasm.

A Single Class

In some schools one teacher introduces philosophical inquiry because of her own interest or perhaps experience at a previous school. This is good for the pupils in that class and can also sometimes act as a catalyst for expansion, as other teachers watch and become interested. From the teacher's perspective, one of the problems of introducing something alone is that there is no one to share with on a professional level. From the student perspective, being in a class in which philosophical inquiry is used and then moving in the next year to a teacher not versed in the methodology is somewhat frustrating. This is because the natural mind-set even after one year is to keep questioning and exploring.

Whole School

When a whole school uses P4C it is the ideal situation for students, teachers and the school itself. Training of staff becomes more cohesive and the student experience can be one of continuous progression. Decisions on whether to place the P4C sessions in a particular curriculum area, or whether to have free-standing enquiries, or a mixture of the two, can be part of the decision-making process of the school. The staff can support each other in this work as they would in other areas. Some schools have a lead teacher who coordinates the program and who becomes the 'go to' person for questions relating to the program.

An internationally known example of a single school development is Buranda School in Queensland, Australia. This school went from being one of the poorest performers in Queensland State tests to being far above the average after taking on a P4C inquiry approach across the school and across the curricular areas. The Alma Mater School in Budapest, Hungary, also took on P4C through the Thinking Through Philosophy program, and has seen many positive changes. In response to their philosophy lessons, one student wrote 'In the Philosophy lesson I have learnt many things: to solve problems, to explore situations in a clever way, to draw conclusions from different situations.' Another said 'The thing is that it can turn my thoughts completely upside down and I will start thinking differently about the same topic. Many times, I think it over and over again for more days.'[1]. The school now regards itself as 'following the philosophical approach' and has started offering training for teachers from other schools. Alma Mater School is fast becoming a beacon school.

Beacon School

A beacon school becomes so either by designation by the school district, or more likely emerges through the efforts and expertise of the teachers of that school. Over a period of time they develop P4C and an inquiry approach within their own school. A beacon school can organize P4C in the area and also take the lead in expertise and so support other schools and classes nearby. This is often on the basis of at least one enthusiastic person.

An example of this approach is Tullynessle Primary School in Aberdeenshire, Scotland[2]. Through the enthusiastic work of the principal, the school developed P4C in all its classes, including the kindergarten. Over several years the principal organized training courses and invited teachers from schools in the area. One of the current authors has trained over 200 teachers in the area over a six-year period because of that initiative. All these teachers had a two-day training course and some follow-up support largely because of the enthusiasm of one person.

The benefits of support that was described for the single school context obviously expands when many schools in an area are operating similar programs. It is also useful when teachers move jobs and can easily fit into the P4C program of the new school. For the students, a bigger program means that there is a more coherent curriculum for those who may move between elementary schools, but is even more important when they transfer to high school or college. Anecdotal evidence from high school teachers was that they were very aware of the more developed linguistic and inquiry skills of students from a P4C background.

The School District Program

At the largest level of development is the introduction of P4C to a whole school district. While this has many benefits, it also has the biggest challenges. An example of this, in which all three current authors were involved, was the Clackmannanshire Project. It took place in a school district (local authority) in Scotland. In the UK the idea of 'thinking skills' was gaining prominence and local education authorities were obliged to address this issue. One of the authors was asked to chair a group of school principals to investigate the issue and plan a way forward for practical introduction of methods into schools. Many different approaches were possible.

The group became convinced that rather than a toolbox type approach, in which particular strategies were linked to particular problems, a more cohesive approach was necessary. This might more easily integrate with the curriculum. Also, around that time, the work of Daniel Goleman[3] in showing the importance of emotional intelligence was becoming popular (although criticized by some academics) and there was some recognition that a P4C approach might also aid social and emotional development. The project introduced philosophical inquiry (P4C) to every school in the district. Initially this was from ages 10 to 12, but later was broadened to include children from kindergarten and also to secondary schools. Later, a DVD on the theory and practice of this approach to philosophical inquiry was produced with funding from the Scottish Government and sent to every school in Scotland.

Having decided on P4C as the best approach, detailed planning was needed to bring it to fruition. Key points were as follows:

- ◆ The project leader spoke to principals, explaining the project and its purpose and asking for any interest from schools in being in the first tranche to be trained. It was felt important that the first group should be principals and teachers who were interested and not coerced into taking part. Their subsequent enthusiasm would be useful in expanding the project later.

- ◆ Training and support of teachers would be important. As project leader, one of the authors took on the task of staff training. Initially this was a one-day course, but later in the project a two-day course was felt more appropriate.

◆ A teacher with experience in philosophical inquiry was employed part-time to support teachers in the project through class visits and practical demonstrations. As a result of this 'trouble-shooting' approach, new methods and practical materials were developed for particular difficulties.

◆ Materials were needed and the 'Thinking Through Philosophy'[4] series of four books was developed and used.

◆ The school district decided that the project should be evaluated and two of the current authors were involved in this, which is described more fully in later chapters.

◆ Continuous student experience was an important consideration. Four grades were in the initial project and two of these were in the evaluation. For logistical reasons it was not possible to train all teachers at once or in the same year. If grade six teachers were in the first year of the project, then the following year those students would have had a year's practice of P4C and would be quite skilled. They would then move to grade seven where the teachers were newly trained and had no experience of P4C and this would likely result in a negative or frustrating experience for the students and also for the teacher. By starting with grade seven in the first year and grade six the next year, this was avoided and the pupil experience was continuous.

◆ Besides a support teacher, a two-hour discussion and training meeting was available to teachers every two or three months. This was useful in sharing successes and addressing difficulties from different schools, as well as developing the pedagogy.

◆ One of the authors has been involved in projects in different countries and in each case, it was thought important to hold a meeting for parents early in the process. There can be many misconceptions when a school announces it is going to begin philosophy sessions, so clarifying these is useful. Also, in some families and local cultures, children asking questions is not encouraged and parents can even be fearful that they will become cheeky and arrogant. Full explanation of the aims and process will soon dispel such notions. Supportive parents, who may over time become participants (through on-going discussion with their children), are very much a force for change.

◆ As a large-scale project proceeds, there is a need for on-going training for new teachers to the school district. New teachers, very often in their first years of teaching, should be specifically catered to and not just expected to 'pick up' the method and program.

◆ Of prime importance for embedding a culture of inquiry in schools across a district is having someone at district level responsible not only for the implementation of the new initiative, but also for its maintenance. Just as at the classroom level teachers were encouraged to keep P4C fresh and innovative, so at district level the same applied. The value the district placed on inquiry-based learning would be reflected in its commitment to properly developing it over time.

A similar but smaller project was carried out in Grenada in the Caribbean. Two consultants worked in all six schools on the two small islands of Carriacou and Petite Martinique. Because of the lack of local expertise to support the project, they ran yearly training visits for three years, training teachers from all schools. On the third visit they built a small team of 'Philosophy Leaders', who could act as advisors within their own schools and as liaison persons. A retired educational psychologist living on Carriacou (who had instigated the program and taken part in the training) acted as a local consultant. The project encountered similar challenges as in the Clackmannanshire Project, but also showed the need for flexibility in planning in order to take account of cultural and social differences.

External Provision of P4C

A different model of how to provide for P4C in schools is where the provision is largely or wholly from outside the school. An excellent example of this comes from Seattle. The University of Washington is a leading United States research center for Philosophy for Children that is involved in philosophy in schools on all levels including teacher and parent education in addition to hosting a philosopher in residence program. Schools in the program, such as John Muir Elementary, have such a position from September through June each year. The responsibilities of the job include contacting the school's teachers at the beginning of the school year to find out the number of philosophy sessions required, and to schedule them. The philosopher-in-residence is responsible for teaching several philosophy sessions each week, with the assistance of the class teachers. She or he also arranges for undergraduates to play a part in the program by assisting in philosophy sessions and then mentoring them in their work in the school. Another important element is the need for continuing connection with parents through the school website and parent newsletter – the PIR does this also. This program seems a very effective way of keeping continuity with a school over a number of years and keeping expertise high and consistent. It overcomes the effect of a constantly changing school staff, as well as maintaining the high profile and importance of Philosophy for Children in the curriculum.

College and Community

In chapter one it was noted that many now view the C in P4C as including colleges and communities – the approach is just as valid for young adults and adults as for children. One of the current authors has been involved in working with Non-Government Agencies (NGOs, effectively charities) in India, where there have been some interesting examples of community participation in philosophical inquiry.

For example, Yerala Project Society (YPS) have not only embedded philosophical inquiry into a secondary school in Jalihal, but have creatively used the P4C method with adults. The first example of the latter is in a small electronics factory, where women who are HIV positive and have no means of support have been given employment. The YPS leader who has been trained in P4C uses the approach to allow the women to talk about their lives. It allows difficulties to come to the fore and be discussed with a view to solving problems. The leader has expressed the view that a more traditional discussion closes people down, whereas philosophical inquiry is much more open. Similarly, the same leader works with teenage girls and their mothers on gender issues and challenging cultural norms. The same effect was noted, where the participants went from not speaking at all to making genuine and open contributions.

An interesting experiment in the wider community was when a YPS teacher, using a 'Thinking Through Philosophy'[4] text in Marathi, had a weekly philosophy session on the community radio station[5]. A story was read out and listeners were invited to telephone with observations and comments during the dialogue section. The radio covered 22 small and very poor villages, but someone always had a phone with which groups could listen to the radio. This was not without its lighter side, as when a farmer called the station after a story with the theme of honesty. He related how the buyer of his buffalo milk had accused him of watering it down, but he was honest and hadn't watered it down. However, forgetting he was on live radio, he went on to say that since he had been accused, he was going to water it down now!

Socio Economic Development Trust (SEDT)[6], another NGO, has begun to use an inquiry approach with a 'curiosity center' they operate for local schools. Many elementary teachers in the area have had some training in P4C, making it more familiar to students when they visit. The center promotes a practical 'hands-on' approach to science, but instead of giving information and knowledge with each piece of equipment, there are questions to stimulate dialogue and discussion. They have to make sense of what they are seeing or doing.

ChaloThinKare Foundation (CTK)[7] is a new NGO that has formed as a result of a Thinking Through Philosophy initiative in Maharashtra state. Its prime function is to introduce philosophical inquiry to schools across India, but it also does community work as well. Inquires are organized within housing associations. Once a week in the evening people from the association can meet together in a community hall and have a philosophical inquiry lead by a trained facilitator. The charity reports great enthusiasm and interest in these sessions.

CTK also works with Tessaturi Monti India[8] to run a staff training module based on philosophical inquiry, which operates for 10 weeks per intake. Tessatura has a factory in Kolhapur that employs over 900 people, producing high-quality shirt fabric. Each group of about 30 people comprises a mixture of management, office staff and machine operators. The module uses P4C to have dialogues about questions from home and work, both philosophical and otherwise. One of the current authors has visited the factory and worked with some of the workforce on such a session. Members of the group expressed amazement at how their improved critical thinking skills affected decisions in life, both at home and work. There was an interest in how this might be available to their children.

These examples of community use of philosophical inquiry give a flavor of the versatility of the method and its relevance to adult and community groups, and show that it is not just for mainstream education.

Conclusion

Philosophical inquiry can take place in many different contexts within an education system and also in many ways within a community. What has been shown here is the great versatility of the method and how it can be used to equal effect in different educational, cultural, social and work situations across all ages. In our next chapter we begin to explore just how P4C has these startling effects.

References

1. Alma Mater School. *The current activities of Alma Mater School of Budapest*. 2018. Available at: http://ujalma.hu [November 1, 2018].
2. Tullynessle Primary School. 2018. Available at: www.tullynessle.aberdeenshire.sch.uk [November 1, 2018].
3. D. Goleman. *Emotional intelligence*. 2014. London: Bloomsbury Publishing.
4. P. Cleghorn. *Thinking through philosophy (Vol. 3)*. 2002. Blackburn, England: Educational Printing Service.
5. Yerala Project Society. 2018. Available at: www.yerala.org [November 1, 2018].
6. Socio Economic Development Trust. 2018. Available at: www.sedtindia.org [November 1, 2018].
7. Chalo ThinKare. 2018. Available at: www.chalothinkare.org/ [March 11, 2019].
8. Tessaturi Monti India. 2018. Available at: www.monti.co.in [November 1, 2018].

5

How Inquiry Promotes More Effective Learning

Teachers will invest more time and energy facilitating philosophical inquiries if they anticipate that this will have a positive and broad effect on their students' learning. This chapter focuses on how and why P4C helps students become more independent thinkers and learners. Thinking and learning are closely intertwined. In order to promote learners who really understand what they are learning, educators need to support and challenge students to think. Students who are able to reflect on learning and thinking processes are likely to be more effective learners than those who do not[1]. We will consider how regular practice in philosophical inquiry encourages such reflection.

How Philosophical Inquiry Improves Learning

Traditionally, educators used external rewards to motivate student behavior. Extrinsically motivated students were rewarded as a consequence of behaving in certain ways that served as a means to an end. However, rewards in themselves do not help students take responsibility for their learning. Rewards are likely to lead to more superficial processing of information that only meets minimal requirements[2].

In contrast, the process of thinking together in philosophical inquiry is likely to encourage intrinsically motivated students. Students become more intrinsically motivated when their needs for personal autonomy, competence and connection are met[3]. Collaborative inquiry provides a means of meeting these needs although this is not its main intention. At any age, intrinsic motivation is seen as more effective than rewards for promoting learning[4].

Intrinsically motivated students are motivated by factors inherent in the task itself. The activity satisfies them or helps make them feel competent. Current theories emphasize that students are motivated by personal goals, competency beliefs and evaluations of their worth rather than external reward. In this context, behavior is motivated by our need to feel competent, autonomous (i.e., having some choice) and being connected to others (i.e., meeting our need for related-ness). Glasser[5] added 'fun' as a fourth psychological need, adding that a repetitive, joyless classroom never inspires students to do regular high-quality work. Learners are most likely to demonstrate energy and persistence and achieve the highest standards when they are intrinsi-cally motivated. As Sullo[6] has argued, personal motivation comes from within: 'External control may lead to compliance but it never inspires you to do your best' (p. 1).

Philosophical Inquiry supports intrinsic motivation and self-regulated behavior because of its emphasis on promoting confi-dent communication and autonomous thinking within an inclusive classroom community. Warm and caring interpersonal relationships are typically among student's highest priorities[7]. Students are more likely to be motivated to learn when they believe their teachers and students respect their views and when they feel that they truly belong to a classroom community[8]. Philosophy for Children encourages intrinsic motivation and supports learning by providing the conditions necessary for meeting students' needs for relatedness and autonomy in their thinking.

Students' beliefs, thoughts and values are now seen as having the main influence on their learning. All of these are regularly examined during philosophical inquiries, as they examine meaningful questions in relation to their own beliefs and values and also in relation to those of others. Philosophy for Children encourages a critical reflection upon such beliefs, including beliefs about ability. Dweck[9] provides a compelling example of how beliefs influence student motivation, investigating how students coped with repeated failure. She suggested that the difference between someone who was determined to master learning challenges and someone who readily gave up lay in their beliefs as to why they failed. Those who believed ability was something that could be cultivated tended to attribute failure to not trying hard enough or to using wrong strategies. They were more likely to persevere and achieve better results in the long run. By contrast, students who were concerned that their failure reflected a 'fixed' unchangeable ability were only confident when the tasks were easy. They would avoid challenging tasks that threatened their self-image. They performed less well when learning became more challenging.

The process of P4C promotes the possibility that the learner's view of themselves changes, and also the views of that learner held by others. The child of ten who cannot write a coherent sentence does think and have ideas. Once supported to contribute ideas into the dialogue, with evidence for that view, the respect of others in the group changes – their view of that person as a learner immediately becomes much more positive. You can see a child grow six inches on the spot! They feel good!

Philosophy for Children provides optimal conditions for examining beliefs and promoting intrinsic motivation. Philosophical inquiry challenges beliefs that are lacking substance (including beliefs relating to learning) and increases awareness of how one thinks and learns. Inquiry supports more effective self-regulation and actively encourages 'metacognition', that is, 'thinking about thinking'. Whereas cognition focus on the products of learning (i.e., the 'what'), metacognition focuses on awareness of the thinking and learning processes that resulted in that knowledge (i.e., the 'how'). Developing metacognitive habits is explicitly encouraged in the philosophical inquiry process. This is important as metacognition lies at the heart of improving learning[10] and is one of the most cost-effective strategies in improving learning[11]. Metacognition is seen as the engine of learning[12].

One characteristic of very able or gifted children it is that they have more metacognitive awareness than their less able peers[13]. Similarly, poor learners have the metacognitive awareness of much younger children[14]. If we can bring the process of learning and thinking to a conscious level (as in philosophical inquiry), we can help students gain control and mastery over the organization of their learning and thinking[15].

At a practical level, facilitators of philosophical inquiry routinely encourage students' metacognitive awareness of thought processes through questions such as:

- ◆ How did we do? What went well? What went less well?
- ◆ How well did listen to each other?
- ◆ Did we respect other's arguments?
- ◆ Did anyone change their minds in response to a reasoned argument from someone else?

Such reflective questions can be applied to the student's own behavior as well as considering the performance of the group as a whole. Over time, increased awareness of behavior will make self-management of behavior more likely, including managing learning strategies.

How Teachers Can Support Students as They Construct Their Thinking and Learning

Philosophy for Children improves learning by providing conditions conducive to intrinsic motivation, productive beliefs and self-management. It encourages a more constructivist approach to teaching. Such an approach is associated with better learning outcomes than classrooms using a traditional transmission model[16]. The constructivist teacher's emphasis is less on 'putting in' (transmitting) knowledge and more on 'drawing out' new knowledge and understanding. A significant weakness of the transmission model is that it encourages dependency on the teacher by the learner. The learner becomes a passive recipient of knowledge and is not encouraged to think critically and creatively as is the case with a more constructivist approach.

When drawing out new knowledge, constructivist teachers check out the student's current understanding of concepts, encourage them to engage in dialogue, ask open-ended questions, encourage students to ask questions, allow thinking time and get students to elaborate their initial responses[2]. This is also a description of Philosophy for Children. Regular participation in philosophical inquiries gives students the opportunity to effectively construct their thinking and learning. However, a constructivist approach is not easy, as teachers can tend to lapse into transmission mode even when they have the best intentions to develop an open, communicative ethos in their classroom[17].

Given such tendencies, it is worth remembering that learning (and philosophical inquiry) is about helping students to construct sense and meaning. Children learn through attempting to make sense of new knowledge by relating it to their existing knowledge. The teacher creates the emotional climate for this to happen in a community of inquiry. Children are social beings who construct their understanding of the world around them by entering into dialogue with others[18]. One person's knowledge can never be identical to another's, because knowledge is the result of a personal interpretation of experience. By engaging with others, learners gain a perspective different from their own. Learning happens when children are required to reorganize their thinking in light of fresh evidence.

Philosophy for Children sets up situations requiring a rethinking of one's position in the light of reasoned argument. According to Piaget[19] such 'cognitive conflict' is an important prerequisite for cognitive development. Cognitive conflict is apparent in thinking programs that result in measurable learning gains, such as Cognitive Acceleration through Science Education (CASE)[20]. The key features of this program were identified as cognitive conflict, social construction (discussed later in this chapter) and metacognition[21]. All three of these features are central to the process of Philosophical Inquiry.

One way that Philosophy for Children helps students to construct thinking and learning is through exploring the meaning of words and concepts during inquiries. Bruner[22] argued that concepts are the fundamental building blocks of our thinking and that people interpret the world in terms of similarities and differences. During philosophical inquiries, the teacher keeps an eye open for opportunities to tease out connections and distinctions between concepts: 'How are these words/ideas connected?' 'How are they different?' Simple practical games and strategies can prepare the ground for productive inquiries. For example, in 'Odd One Out'[23], teachers present young students with a picture of a hen, a frog and a duck. Students then choose an odd one out and give a reason, e.g., the frog is the odd one out because it does not have feathers. Odd One Out helps children make connections, enabling more accurate definitions through creating examples and counter-examples. The same strategy can be used to clarify concepts of increasing complexity, ambiguity and nuance.

Thinking through Philosophy also aims to encourage students to think more critically and views this as an important function of education. Learning is seen as more than simple retention. Good teachers do not just teach subject content, they teach thinking. They stimulate learners by encouraging them to question and reflect. What Dewey[24] referred to as 'reflection' would now be more typically referred to as critical thinking. However, promoting critical thinking through Philosophical Inquiry only fulfills this purpose of education if skills transfer beyond the immediate inquiry.

Transfer Across Subject Boundaries and Beyond

Teachers will feel more confident committing time and energy to philosophical inquiry if improvements in thinking are found to transfer across subject boundaries. Maximizing the transfer of learning beyond the context in which it is learned is at the heart of the matter[25].

The question of transfer of thinking skills remains contentious. Some philosophers argue that thinking can only take place in particular contexts, while others believe that elements of any new thinking have the potential to be generalized to new and similar situations. Contrasting views over this issue have been explored[26], one view emphasizing the centrality of subject-specific knowledge, the other the generalizability of critical thinking skills. Focusing on Philosophy for Children, Sutcliffe[17] took the view that one's practice of thinking can be transferred from one discipline to another, while acknowledging that those with knowledge of a particular discipline will be better at thinking within that discipline.

Transfer of learning beyond the context in which it is learned is more likely to occur if activities are built in to transfer that learning to other contexts. Adey and Shayer[20] maximized transfer by building in 'bridging' activities to transfer learning beyond the immediate context. They found that thinking gains in science successfully transferred to improved learning outcomes in English and mathematics. Building in transfer activities was also central to the thinking gains arising from Feuerstein's Instrumental Enrichment program[27].

Similarly, 'bridging' activities were explicitly built into the Thinking Through Philosophy program[28], so that thinking during philosophical inquiries transferred to children's lives outside the classroom inquiries. This program resulted in gains in reasoning ability in eleven- and twelve-year-olds[29]. Importantly, the cognitive ability of eleven-year-olds is highly correlated with their subsequent performance in national academic tests when they are aged sixteen[30]. Transfer may also be apparent in teacher behavior as well as student learning. Anecdotal evidence[31] suggested that elementary school teachers tended to transfer the practice of inquiry to other subjects outside the 'philosophy hour'. After all, Philosophy for Children refers to inquiry that can be applied to any subject. Besides the teachers consciously moving to a more inquiry-based method, many teachers notice that the students themselves naturally began to ask more and better questions in other subject areas. Transfer can also be achieved when an inquiry is used as part of another curricular area, such as to start a historical project.

Challenging Themes: An Example Beyond the Curriculum

How can P4C address challenging contemporary themes that go beyond the narrow confines of the curriculum? An example would be to use P4C to address the issue of climate change. In this you could use the critical thinking tool 'Spectrum of Meaning' available in the book's Resource Website (see Download 14). One end of the Spectrum would be labeled Fact and the other end Opinion.

To introduce the subject, a paragraph from an imaginary news report can be read: 'At a recent international conference on climate change held in Geneva, the Prime Minister of the tiny Pacific island of Tuvalu explained how his home will be very much affected by climate change in the future. Tuvalu comprises a group of nine coral atolls totaling ten square miles and none rises more than 4.5 meters above the sea. "Our beautiful islands are disappearing under the sea", he said.'

Have a brainstorming session where the question is 'What *is* climate change?' Take all ideas and write them on the board. Use the connections and tensions technique to connect the ideas, with students giving reasons for these. Then put the students into pairs and give them the task of searching for articles and information regarding climate change using the classification 'Fact' or 'Opinion'. Have them consider why people might have different views on this subject. Each pair should choose one (short) idea, article or paragraph as especially interesting.

Then make groups of four by putting two of the previous pairs together. Each pair should explain their piece of evidence to the other pair. Once this is complete bring the whole class together again. Using 'Fact' and 'Opinion' for the poles of the spectrum, have each pair consider where on the spectrum their item of interest might be placed with regards to scientific evidence for climate change. Each pair should tell the group briefly what their evidence is about and physically place it on the spectrum *giving a reason/evidence for placing it in that position.* For closure, students can give their final position on causes of climate change. Has their opinion moved as a result of the activity?

Higher-Order Thinking

Thus, students move beyond the curriculum to consider multi-disciplinary issues that loom large in the real lives of everyone – maybe not today, but at some point in the future. Higher-order thinking is certainly used. Philosophical inquiries support learning through promoting intrinsic motivation, practicing metacognition strategies, challenging unproductive beliefs, encouraging 'cognitive conflict', facilitating the social 'construction' of knowledge and building bridging activities to transfer skills to other contexts. When students are required to use these higher-order thinking skills, their academic achievement improves[32]. It is therefore important that teachers press their students to think in ways that adds depth to their understanding of whatever they are learning about. Philosophical inquiry encourages such habits.

Higher-order thinking is required when the student's path of action is not fully specified in advance and often yields multiple solutions rather than unique solutions. This thinking is evident in philosophical inquiry. Such thinking involves nuanced judgments and interpretation and often involves uncertainty. Higher-order thinking requires imposing meaning through finding structure in apparent disorder and is therefore effortful[33].

The effortful nature of higher-order thinking resembles the slower, conscious and more logical 'System 2' thinking[34] described by Kahneman, rather than his instinctive and emotional System 1 thinking. Kahneman suggested our brains are hardwired to react to certain cues with System 1 thinking to help us survive. This implies that we need to work hard to develop habits of higher-order thinking to counter more instinctive, emotional responses. The more-conscious thinking process (as encouraged by the awareness exercise) allows any emotional aspect of a question to be part of the cognitive consideration. Re-educating our habits though practicing thinking together, as in philosophical inquiry, aims to sway the balance in the competition between System 1 and System 2 thinking. Swaying this balance towards self-regulation encourages more effective learning strategies.

Higher-order thinking implies a hierarchy of thinking akin to Bloom's Taxonomy[35] developed back in the 1950s. Bloom's Taxonomy provides a classification of thinking skills to be used as a tool to help teachers broaden their view of student learning beyond the simple recall of information. That classification places critical and creative thinking at the top of the hierarchy. Although updated[36], Bloom's Taxonomy has remained influential as a reminder that students need to process and apply their learning in order for that learning to be fully effective. In the context of Philosophy for Children, Lipman[37] argued for a non-hierarchical approach to thinking and learning (i.e., each level is equally important) and some educators[2] now prefer the less hierarchical term 'complex thinking skills' to 'higher-order thinking'. The crucial point is not whether one process is more important that another, but that it is in the interests of the learner to develop habits of thoroughly processing the information they are considering rather than seeking to simply retain that information. Philosophical inquiry provides a means of encouraging such habits and considers the student's level of development and sophistication in this process.

Communities Support Learning

'Social construction' involves students engaging in group discussion to solve problems or deepen understandings. Social construction was identified as a necessary feature of programs that improve learning through developing thinking abilities[21]. This implies that the majority of students think more productively when they are engaged in groups that share common goals and values.

Sharing common goals and values is also a central idea of learning communities. A learning community has been described as a collective that learns together and includes a focus on building social as well as learning relations. In this context, Watkins[12] provided the following quote from an eleven-year old that nicely captures the social aspect of learning: 'Even if you learn something perfectly, or are a pioneer in your area, all your work is useless if nobody else can understand you. You might as well have done no work at all. The point of learning is to share it with others' (p. 5).

Schools whose practices derive from thinking of the school as a community get higher academic performance[38]. This applies to both elementary schools[39] and high schools[40]. Academic motivation and achievement can be increased by strengthening a sense of a community of learners, as in the Child Development Project[41]. At schools high in 'community' (as measured by the degree of students' agreement with statements such as 'My school is like a family' and 'Students really care about each other'), students show higher educational expectations and academic performance. Students with a higher sense of school belonging report higher grades and an increased sense that success is more in their hands than in the hands of others[42]. The strongest positive effects of school community have occurred among schools with the most disadvantaged student populations[43].

Regular participation in Philosophy for Children aims to gradually build a 'community of inquiry' sharing several features of the learning communities described above. Both emphasize inclusiveness, participation and social solidarity. However, a community of inquiry goes beyond the concept of a learning community in its emphasis on a communal quest for meaning through building on each other's ideas and reasoned discussion[37]. The important point is that Philosophy for Children shares the features of programs found to be effective in improving learning. Thinking together is encouraged to construct a better understanding than would be possible on one's own. Participation in Philosophy for Children mirrors the sense of belonging found in learning communities that benefit student learning. However, a community of inquiry goes well beyond the concept of a learning community though its emphasis on developing critical thinking.

Theoretical Perspectives

This chapter has aimed to connect philosophical inquiry to classroom practices associated with improved learning outcomes. This book emphasizes a practical method for engaging students in reasoned discussion that is structured yet rich in spontaneity. However, it is also relevant to add a brief note on the theoretical perspectives that underpin this method. Philosophy for Children is not a 'stand-alone' approach, but a process that resonates with accumulated knowledge from many fields about how students develop their thinking and learning.

Philosophical inquiry is rooted in philosophical pragmatism that contends that knowledge is the product of inquiry. It follows John Dewey's tradition of reflective education, whereby learning to think is a primary aim of education. Dewey's concept of reflective learning can be viewed as synonymous with critical thinking. Matthew Lipman, the originator of Philosophy for Children, was a student of Dewey's at Columbia University, and saw philosophical inquiry as a means of developing critical thinking (and the other three Cs discussed in Chapter 2).

Reference has already been made in the preceding chapters to the work of cognitive psychologists such as Vygotsky, Bruner and Piaget, and how their contributions fit with students' developing their thinking in philosophical inquiry. Lipman[37] drew inspiration from the Russian psychologist, Vygotsky. Consistent with Vygotskian thinking, Lipman recognized that members of a community of inquiry internalize the social practices of the community. So, for example, initially members request reasons of each other, before internalizing that behavior to routinely reflect on reasons for their own thinking. Similarly, members are encouraged to build on one another's ideas, then build on their own ideas. The habits of thinking that start out distributed around the group become internalized within the individual. The process of Philosophy for Children thus enacts Vygotsky's ideas as to how children develop cognitively.

Vygotsky also proposed that, with support, children can typically do more difficult things in collaboration with an adult or an abler peer than they can do on their own. The range of tasks that children could not yet perform independently but could perform with support of an adult is their Zone of Proximal Development (ZPD). Similarly, with the support and challenge of a community of inquiry, students can typically construct more meaningful interpretations than they could achieve on their own.

Jerome Bruner further developed Vygotsky's work. Bruner's metaphorical term 'scaffolding' refers to the support, often in the form of dialogue, from an adult or abler peer, that maximizes the learning and thinking capabilities of a student[44]. Consistent with the practice of Philosophy for Children, scaffolding includes the gradual withdrawal of adult support as the student becomes more proficient in the inquiry process.

In some ways Piaget's theory of cognitive development runs counter to Philosophy for Children. Piaget's theory suggests that students are only capable of formal abstract thinking in adolescence, but philosophical inquiry has routinely demonstrated that younger children, given appropriate support, are fully capable of a reasoned exploration of abstract concepts. One area of Piaget's work that *is* consistent with the process of philosophical inquiry is his concept of 'disequilibrium'[19]. Disequilibrium occurs when a student is unable to respond to new events or information because these events fail to fit in with existing understandings. This results in 'cognitive conflict'. For Piaget the idea of cognitive conflict was an important element in cognitive development and recognized the potential contribution of peer interaction to this process.

Later neo-Piagetian concepts of sociocognitive conflict[45] strengthened the role of peer social contexts in generating cognitive conflict. In philosophical inquiry, sociocognitive conflict is likely to arise during the course of discussion in a community of inquiry as ideas and beliefs are challenged by others who support contrasting views with reasons and evidence. This leads to cognitive development. In this sense, learning is the result of an intrinsic drive to resolve inconsistencies and contradictions and to have a view of the world that makes sense in the light of what we already know. Inquiry is a meaning-making process.

Summary

This chapter has considered how philosophical inquiry strengthens learning: the number one priority for educators. The regular practice of collaborative inquiry in the classroom strengthens learning through encouraging intrinsic motivation, self-regulation, metacognition, the active social construction of learning, promoting classroom communities of learning and thinking, building in challenge and transfer, sharpening conceptual connections and distinctions and requiring deeper processing of what is being learned. In short, philosophical inquiry should not be seen as an extra to the business of schools, but as providing a means for greater long-term gains in learning in all subjects across the curriculum. The chapter offers a final note on how philosophical inquiry is consistent with major psychological perspectives on how students develop cognitively and educationally.

References

1. L. Meltzer. *Executive function in education: From theory to practice*. 2007. New York, NY: Guilford Press.
2. J. E. Ormrod. *Essentials of educational psychology*. 2009. Upper Saddle River, NJ: Pearson.
3. E. L. Deci and R. M. Ryan. *Intrinsic motivation and self-determination in human behavior*. 1985. New York, NY: Plenum Press.
4. A. Kohn. *Feel-bad education and other contrarian essays on children and schooling*. 2011. Boston, MA: Beacon Press.
5. W. Glasser. *Choice theory: A new psychology of personal freedom*. 1998. New York, NY: HarperCollins.
6. B. Sullo. *Activating the desire to learn*. 2007. Alexandria, VA: Association for Supervision and Curriculum Development.
7. J. Juvonen. Sense of belonging, social bonds, and school functioning. In: P. A. Alexander & P. H. Winne (Eds.) *Handbook of educational psychology*. 2006, pp. 655–674. Mahwah, NJ: Erlbaum.
8. C. Furrer and E. Skinner. Sense of relatedness as a factor in children's academic engagement and performance. *Journal of Educational Psychology*, 2003, vol. 95, issue 1, pp. 148–162.
9. C. Dweck. *Self theories: Their role in motivation, personality and development*. 2000. Florence, KY: Psychology Press.
10. R. J. Marazano. *A theory-based meta-analysis of research on instruction*. 1998. Aurora, CO: McREL.
11. S. Higgins. *Thinking through primary teaching*. 2002. Cambridge, England: Chris Kington.
12. C. Watkins. Classrooms as learning communities. *National school improvement network bulletin*, Autumn 2004, issue 24, pp. 1–8.
13. R. Sternberg and J. E. Davidson. Insight in the gifted. *Educational Psychologist*, 1983, vol. 18, pp. 51–57.
14. J. Campione. Metacognitive components of instructional research with problem learners. In: F. Weinert and R. Kluwer (Eds.) *Metacognition, motivation and understanding*. 1987, pp. 117–140. Hillsdale, NJ: LEA.
15. J. H. Flavell. Metacognition and cognitive monitoring: a new area of cognitive-developmental inquiry. *American Psychologist*, October 1979, vol. 34, no. 10, pp. 906–911.
16. F. C. Staub and E. Stern. The nature of teachers' pedagogical content beliefs matters for students' achievement gains. *Journal of Educational Psychology*, 2002, vol. 94, pp. 344–355.

17. R. Sutcliffe. Is teaching philosophy a high road to cognitive enhancement? *Educational and Child Psychology*, 2003, vol. 20, issue 2, pp. 65–79.

18. L. S. Vygotsky. *Thought and language* (translation of Vygotsky's original 1934 publication in Russian '*Myshlenie i rech*'). 1962. Cambridge, MA: MIT Press.

19. J. Piaget and B. Inhelder. *The psychology of the child.* 1969. New York, NY: Basic Books.

20. P. Adey and M. Shayer. *Really raising standards: Cognitive intervention and academic achievement.* 1994. London: Routledge.

21. M. Shayer and P. Adey (Eds.) *Learning intelligence: Cognitive acceleration across the curriculum from 5 to 15 years.* 2002. Buckingham: Open University Press.

22. J. Bruner et al. *A study of thinking.* 1967. New York, NY: Wiley.

23. S. Higgins. *Developing thinking skills in the primary classroom.* Paper presented at the Conference on Raising Achievement, University College, Worcester, October 27, 2001. Available at: http://www.leeds.ac.uk/educol/documents/140953.htm [November 1, 2018].

24. J. Dewey. My pedagogic creed. *The School Journal*, 1897, LIV vol. 3, pp. 77–80.

25. C. McGuinness. *From thinking skills to thinking classrooms.* 1999. London: Department for Education and Employment.

26. S. Bailin and H. Siegel. Critical thinking. In: N. Blake et al. (Eds.) *The Blackwell guide to the philosophy of education.* 2003, pp. 181–193. Oxford, UK: Blackwell.

27. R. Feuerstein et al. *Instrumental Enrichment: An intervention programme for cognitive modifiability.* 1980. Baltimore, MD: University Park Press.

28. P. Cleghorn. *Thinking through philosophy.* 2002. Blackburn, England: Educational Printing Services.

29. K. J. Topping and S. Trickey. Collaborative philosophical enquiry for school children: Cognitive effects at 10–12 years. *British Journal of Educational Psychology*, 2007, issue 77, pp. 271–288.

30. I. J. Deary et al. Intelligence and educational achievement. *Intelligence*, 2007, vol. 35, issue 1, pp. 13–21.

31. S. Trickey and K. J. Topping. Collaborative philosophical enquiry for school children: Participant evaluation at 11 years. *Thinking: The Journal of Philosophy for Children*, 2007, vol. 18, issue 3, pp. 23–34.

32. H. Wenglinsky. Facts or critical thinking skills? What NAEP results say. *Educational Leadership*, 2004, vol. 62, issue 1, pp. 32–35.

33. L. Resnick. *Education and learning to think.* 1997. Washington, DC: National Academy Press.

34. D. Kahneman. *Thinking, fast and slow.* 2011. New York, NY: Farrer, Straus & Giroux.

35. B. S. Bloom et al. *Taxonomy of educational objectives: The classification of educational goals. Handbook I: Cognitive domain.* 1956. New York: David McKay Company.

36. L. W. Anderson and D. R. Krathwohl (Eds.) *A taxonomy for learning, teaching and assessing: A revision of Bloom's taxonomy of educational objectives.* 2001. New York, NY: Longman.

37. M. Lipman. *Thinking in education.* 2003. Cambridge, England: Cambridge University Press.

38. J. E. Zins et al. (Eds.). *Building academic success on social and emotional learning: What does the research say?* 2004. New York, NY: Columbia University.

39. C. C. Lewis, E. Schaps and M. S. Watson. The caring classroom's academic edge. *Educational Leadership*, 1996, vol. 54, issue 1, pp. 16–21.

40. V. E. Lee and J. B. Smith. Effects of high school restructuring and size on early gains in achievement and engagement. *Sociology of Education*, 1995, vol. 68, issue 4, pp. 241–270.

41. E. Schaps, V. Battistich and D. Solomon. Community in school as key to student growth: Findings from the Child Development Project. In: J. E. Zins et al. (Eds.) *Building academic success on social and emotional learning: What does the research say?* 2004, pp. 189–205. New York, NY: Columbia University.

42. W. Hagborg. An investigation of a brief measure of school membership. *Adolescence,* 1998, issue 20, pp. 525–535.

43. V. Battistich. Schools as communities, poverty levels of student populations, and students' attitudes, motives, and performance: A multilevel analysis. *American Educational Research Journal*, 1995, vol. 32, issue 3, pp. 627–658.

44. D. J. Wood, J. S. Bruner and G. Ross. The role of tutoring in problem solving. *Journal of Child Psychiatry and Psychology*, 1976, vol. 17, issue 2, pp. 89–100.

45. W. Doise and G. Mugny. *The social development of the intellect.* 1984. Oxford: Pergamon.

6

Educating Students to Think: The Contribution of Philosophical Inquiry

As Michael (aged 10) said during the course of a P4C discussion, 'Thinking is very hard to explain'. If a teacher were to ask a group of fifth grade students, 'What is thinking?' they would be likely to receive a wide range of answers. The authors did just this[1]. In addition to Michael's comment, other responses included:

- When you have a picture in your head of something
- When you really concentrate on something and open your mind
- When you put your mind to something and come up with a suitable answer.

The range of answers proved too wide to group student responses into meaningful categories for statistical analysis. Halpern has suggested[2] (p. 4) that 'unfortunately there are no satisfactory definitions of thinking' and that definitions of thinking are arbitrary. That has not stopped many attempts. The cognitive psychologist, Jerome Bruner, defined thinking as 'going beyond the information given' (used as a title of his book[3]). Going back over a century, the philosopher John Dewey, stated[4] (p. 13) that thinking was 'to maintain the state of doubt and to carry on systematic and protracted inquiry'. The last definition's link between thinking and inquiry seems appropriate for this book.

What Are Some of the Issues Around Teaching Thinking?

Although the notion of thinking 'skills' that can be taught has been seen by some[5] as contentious, others[6,7] have sought to analyze thinking into more specific component skills that can be developed in educational contexts. These skills become interdependent in real-life problem solving. A list of such skills follows to show the specific thinking abilities that are relevant to Thinking Through Philosophy:

- ◆ Sequencing and ordering information
- ◆ Sorting, classifying and grouping of information
- ◆ Defining problems
- ◆ Asking relevant questions
- ◆ Comparing and contrasting
- ◆ Hypothesizing
- ◆ Giving reasons and evidence to support opinions
- ◆ Drawing conclusions based on evidence
- ◆ Defining and clarifying problems
- ◆ Evaluating outcomes
- ◆ Finding alternative explanations for a conclusion.

There has also been a long-standing debate as to whether thinking skills can be taught independently of a specific subject. One view[8] would be to argue that students need to have a knowledge of history in order to think critically about history. Conversely, advocates of Philosophy for Children[9] take the view that thinking derived through inquiry can be generalized to some degree to other subjects, although exercising these skills fully demands additional domain-specific knowledge. Philosophical concepts, such as fairness, love and greed, are seen as providing an effective stimulus for thinking because of their ambiguity. The issue of whether thinking can be taught independently of subjects is of significance to teachers due to the role of higher-order thinking in enhancing learning. This debate mirrors the issue of 'transfer', mentioned in the last chapter. The nurturing of critical thinking remains a fundamental aim of Philosophy for Children. While teaching critical thinking is not straightforward[10], philosophical inquiry can contribute to critical thinking[11] and we assert that the method can be applied to the teaching of other subjects[12,13,14].

Why Promote Thinking and Problem Solving in the Classroom?

There are many reasons why teachers want to educate their students to think. The intimate connection between thinking and learning was considered in the previous chapter. We will also consider how thinking can help to regulate emotions (see Chapter 7) and promote citizenship through democratic participation (Chapter 10). The ability to think for oneself and be able to solve problems is valued by employers[15]. Employees need to think critically, be creative, solve problems, collaborate and communicate more effectively[16]. This profile is consistent with skills to be nurtured in a community of inquiry. According to one analysis[17], mentions for critical thinking in job postings doubled between 2009 and 2014. Most of the jobs needed now did not exist in the past and in future we will need employment skills that do not exist today[18].

Problem solving skills require both critical thinking and creative thinking. In practice, critical thinking and creative thinking are indivisible[19]. While critical thinking is viewed as analytic and evaluative and creative thinking as generative, both are needed in problem solving. Creative thinking creates the possibilities that must then be critically evaluated for effective problem solving. While there are other ways[20] that teachers can infuse critical thinking and creative thinking into curricular content, philosophical inquiry provides teachers with a process that can potentially be applied across the curriculum[12,13,14].

Critical Thinking

Reference has been made to a key aim of Philosophy for Children – that of developing students' critical thinking. It is important to clarify what we mean by critical thinking. There are several definitions of critical thinking[21,22,23]. These definitions share a consensus regarding the key features. These are largely captured in Beyer's[24] definition of critical thinking, which is the ability to assess the authenticity, accuracy, and/or worth of knowledge claims and arguments. In the classroom, the student who thinks critically not only justifies what she or he is saying with reasons, but also is disposed habitually to think in this way. Critical thinking is disciplined thinking that a person uses to evaluate and judge the validity of something (such as statements, news stories, arguments, research, etc.).

The American Philosophical Association[23] identified six skills underpinning critical thinking:

1. Interpretation, including the need for information to be categorized and for meanings to be clarified,
2. Analysis, including the examination of ideas and the analysis of arguments, for example, what reasons support a conclusion,
3. Evaluation, involving assessing the level of confidence to place on a claim or argument and assessing arguments to see if there are any weaknesses in the argument,
4. Inference, referring to the strength of the conclusions, formulating alternative explanations and drawing out any presuppositions,
5. Explanation, providing a justification of one's reasoning in terms of the evidence and methodology, and
6. Self-regulation, requiring awareness of one's own thought processes, detecting one's biases and being able to correct as necessary.

In order to routinely distinguish fact from opinion, the learner needs not only skills such as the above, but the inclination, or disposition, to use these skills on a regular basis. A disposition to critical thinking includes listening to another person's argument with open-mindedness but guarded skepticism. The ideal critical thinker is habitually inquisitive, well-informed, trustful of reason, flexible, fair-minded in evaluation, honest in facing personal biases, prudent in making judgments, willing to reconsider, diligent in seeking relevant information, focused in inquiry and persistent in seeking results. That ideal is a lot to ask for! However, educating critical thinkers means moving in this direction.

From early childhood, children should be taught to reason, to seek relevant facts and to understand the views of others. The disposition for critical thinking needs nurturing. Philosophical inquiry provides a structured process to encourage such behaviors. Critical thinking is not an add-on but an essential aspect of the entire learning-teaching process. Student awareness as to what extent conclusions are based on evidence is an integral part of the Common Core State Standards. For example, the objective[25] that students 'delineate and evaluate the argument and specific claims in a text, assessing whether the reasoning is valid and the evidence is relevant and sufficient; identify false statements and fallacious reasoning' resonates perfectly with Thinking Through Philosophy.

It is easy to jump to conclusions based on inadequate information. When asked to justify an opinion, more than half the United States population flounder[26]. The problem is that they lack a grasp of the notion of evidence. Critical thinking challenges our tendency to make evidence subservient to emotive belief and inbuilt bias. For example, the belief that that the United States population would be more secure if people from some Muslim countries were refused entry is not supported by evidence[27]. Between September 2001 and January 2017 not a single American was killed in a terrorist attack by a citizen from the countries in question. Conversely, an American was at least twice as likely to be shot dead by a toddler than killed by a terrorist[28]. But such beliefs once established are not easily overturned because of the nature of confirmation bias.[29] While it is beyond the scope of this book to provide extensive examples of cognitive bias, Richard Nesbitt's book, *Mindware*[30], is rich in such examples, together with what can be done to counter that tendency. One way to avoid errors in thinking is to think more critically. Philosophical inquiry pushes students to do this.

Which Students Do We Teach to Think?

Teachers might think on the basis of Bloom's hierarchical model that only more able students benefit from developing critical thinking. However, a more important factor in successfully developing thinking appears to be the opinion of the teacher[31]. Existing research[32] suggests that high intellectual ability in students is neither a necessary nor a sufficient condition for successful thinking. Nevertheless, up to 40% of middle school and high school teachers reported that instruction on critical thinking skills was not appropriate for lower ability students[33]. This runs counter to the observations of teachers who have engaged in philosophical inquiry with young elementary and mixed-ability high school students. In Philosophy for Children, no child is ever excluded.

An Introduction to Logical Reasoning Skills

Philosophy for Children involves students searching together for truth both in school and real-life settings – and this requires reasoning. In general, we consider something to be true if the available evidence seems to verify it. In searching for the truth, philosophical inquiry aims to encourage students to think logically, so that their reasoning becomes the basis for inferring a valid conclusion. Reasoning can be inductive or deductive.

Inductive reasoning is a thinking process in which one uses specific examples to arrive at a generalization. It involves identifying patterns and forming hypotheses about a general rule or statement. For example, if we observe every morning that the sun rises in the east, we would conclude that it always rises in the east. Analogy is a form of inductive reasoning that notes that when two or more things are similar in some respects, they are probably also similar in some further respect. If someone wants to persuade a friend to watch a movie they enjoyed, the easiest way to persuade them may be to compare the movie to other movies that they have watched. In inductive reasoning (from the specific to the general) observations are collected that support a conclusion. In the number sequence of 1, 2, 6, 24, 120, inductive reasoning can be used to hypothesize the next number.

While one can never be certain with inductive reasoning, the number of previous instances helps to determine the strength of the inductive inference. Inductive reasoning is less strong in the case of a creationist who likens the universe to a watch. As both the universe and a watch are complicated, the creationist might reason that neither could have come about by accident and therefore both must have been created by someone. You can never prove that your statement or hypothesis is correct through inductive reasoning. However, you can disprove it by finding an exception to the rule.

The limitations of inductive reasoning are vividly shown in an example given by Strong, Hanson and Silver[34] that tells the story of a group of young children lost in the woods who need a fire to stay warm. They came across various objects and noted that tree limbs, dowels, chair legs and pencils burned. The next day the children used their generalization that only cylindrical objects burn and collected pieces of pipe, some bottles and an axle from an old car, while discarding a large box of newspapers and some flat wooden boards. Their initial generalization had been reasonable until they found exceptions to the rule.

In contrast to inductive reasoning, in deductive reasoning the student makes inferences using a general rule to make a specific conclusion. Syllogistic reasoning is a form of reasoning in which two statements (a major and a minor premise) are made and a logical conclusion is drawn from them. An example would be:

All children like candy.
Mary is a child.
Therefore, Mary likes candy.

However, the premises have to be true to guarantee the conclusion. A critically thinking student might identify a fallacy in this argument by saying, 'But I know a child who does not like candy.'

Logical deductive reasoning can be extended to abstract concepts as in the question[35]: If some slurms are marsts, and if some marsts are borfs, then are some slurms borfs? Are some borfs marsts?

Words or concepts can be related in one of only three ways (two of which are illustrated above). By concentrating on sentences that capture these relationships, Aristotle developed a framework for clearer thinking. In one of Matthew Lipman's original Philosophy for Children novels[36], he created a story to show Harry Stottlemeier reasoning out these relationships, so that he was able to make a logically consistent argument free from fallacies (chapter 1, p. 3–4).

And then Harry had an idea. 'A sentence can't be reversed. If you put the last part first, it'll no longer be true. For example, take the sentence "All oaks are trees." If you turn it around, it becomes "All trees are oaks." But that's false. Now it's true that "All planets revolve around the sun." But if you turn the sentence around and say "All things that revolve around the sun are planets," then it's no longer true – it's false!' Harry was thrilled with his discovery.

Mrs. Olsen was saying, 'Let me tell you something Mrs. Stottlemeier. That Mrs. Bates, who just joined the PTA, every day I see her go into the liquor store. Now, you know how concerned I am about those unfortunate people who just can't stop drinking. Every day I see them go into the liquor store. Well, that makes me wonder whether Mrs. Bates is, you know...' Suddenly something in Harry's mind went 'click!' 'Mrs. Olsen', he said, 'just because, according to you, all people who can't stop drinking are people who go into a liquor store, that doesn't mean that all people who go into a liquor store are people who can't stop drinking.' ...Harry could tell by the expression on his mother's face that she was pleased with what he'd said. A logical argument is one in which, if the basic facts are true, the conclusion that follows should also be true.

While having a grasp of basic logical relationships has its uses, it would be a mistake to perceive critical thinking skills as limited to spotting logical fallacies[37]. Socrates, Plato and Aristotle have been referred to as the Greek 'gang of three', whose emphasis on logic and analysis is seen as coming at the expense of creative thinking. However, it has also been argued[38] that we should not undervalue analysis and argument in good judgment. In Thinking Through Philosophy, critical thinking is dialogical, requires a disposition to think and emphasizes creative and caring thinking as well as logical reasoning. A final thought to 'clarify' logic comes from Lewis Carroll[39] in *Through the Looking-Glass* (Chapter 4): '"Contrariwise," continued Tweedledee, "if it was so, it might be; and if it were so, it would be; but as it isn't, it ain't. That's logic."'

Creative Thinking

Effective thinking and problem solving not only require logical analytic thinking but also creative thinking. Despite Matthew Lipman's emphasis on the need for creative thinking in Philosophy for Children, P4C has still occasionally been seen as overly logical[40]. In order to problem solve, we need to think creatively as well as critically. We need to think (divergently) of possibilities before evaluating which alternative is likely to be the most productive (convergent thinking). Creative thinkers are able to think *fluently*, coming up with ideas with ease; *flexibly*, seeing things though different perspectives; *originally*, coming up with ideas that are novel, and *elaborately*, building upon ideas[41].

In the same way that teachers can use warm up activities such as Odd One Out (Chapter 5) to start students thinking critically, teachers can use a range of activities to encourage students to practice thinking creatively. Fluency can be practiced through activities such as 'Write down how many non-standard uses of a brick can you think of in two minutes.' Responses can also be rated for originality.

Flexibility can be encouraged by riddles such as the classic 'You are walking through a desert and find a man lying face down with a pack on his back. How did he die?' Students are instructed that in order to solve this problem, they can only ask their teacher questions that can be responded to with 'Yes' or 'No'. Solving problems such as these becomes like solving scientific problems, in that both involve making sense of contradictory data. In both riddles and science problems, there is a need to view the data from as many perspectives as possible and avoid prior assumptions, for example, assuming that the man was carrying a backpack. Only then can a solution to the riddle be found, in this case, that he jumped out of an airplane, but his parachute failed to open. Students need to be taught to look for the assumptions in arguments, such as 'There is nothing wrong with talking on a cell phone in class because other students do it all the time'. Students might identify that this assumes that if an action is done by other students all the time, there is nothing wrong with it.

Identifying assumptions is a creative thinking process, that is, one cannot separate critical and creative thinking. The parachute problem created different ideas and possibilities from a single starting scenario of a man found in the desert. This would be an example of divergent thinking. At the end of the process students had to analyze the information available to decide a single solution, i.e. convergent thinking. Questions encouraging creative thinking can be used as a warm up activity to philosophical inquiry. Examples include:

What if clouds rained happiness?
What if everyone was alike? (no diversity.)
What would happen if there were no hills?
The answer is 'the current president of the United States'. What is the question?
How is a book like a river?

Similarly, creative thinking is encouraged through more complex questions such as: 'If there had been colonist representation in parliament when arguing against taxation without representation, how might the United States be different today?' or 'If illegal drugs were legalized, then…'

These activities also potentially provide practice for thinking about solutions to more complex contemporary issues, such world climate change or 'nationalism vs. globalization'. Teachers need to press students to critically analyze their responses to avoid them merely being 'personal opinions'. Questions, such as 'Can you explain to me why?' can probe and seek clarification from students of all ages. Not only do students need to provide evidence supporting their hypotheses, but also need to be alert to counter-examples that could negate their hypothesis. Hypotheses generated from 'If... then' statements, like the one above, provide particularly fertile ground for creative and critical thinking.

For example, if the stimulus is a story or poem, then when reading it to the class there will be many opportunities to ask 'Why?' when an event or something of importance happens. Gaining a wide range of answers and not accepting any as correct encourages students to keep thinking – creatively. Secondly, Stage 2 of the process, the listing of themes then drawing connections and tensions, is specifically designed to promote creative thinking. More than one link can be drawn between any two or more ideas, provided that for each link a different reason is given. When the creativity is flowing the board ends up looking like a mass of neural connections! This process also provides an example of how creative thinking can lead to deeper and perhaps more critical thinking later, since the evidence of many links inevitably leads to a deeper philosophical dialogue.

This idea of always looking at a range of ideas can also be useful in general classroom management. Whenever there is an incident to be dealt with or even discussion about something from outside school, questions such as 'How else could this have been dealt with?', 'Are there different options?', and 'What are the consequences for different actions?' are readily taken up by students with a range of solutions.

Intelligent Students!

If teachers are asked what student classroom behaviors would lead them to consider some students as 'intelligent' students, they might include students who are curious and questioning, able to connect ideas, are engaged and able to think for themselves. The question might also be asked as to whether philosophical inquiry contributes to students' intelligence. This question needs to consider what is meant by 'intelligence' and whether intelligence can be developed through environmental experiences[42] such as classroom dialogue. Although this book will not attempt to repeat the environment vs. hereditary debate about intelligence, it has practical significance for teachers.

Some investigators[43,44,45] have historically concluded that genes rigidly limit children's capacity to develop intellectually and argued that educational programs aiming to develop cognitive abilities are a waste of time. Some of this work has been shown[46] to be seriously flawed or been vigorously riposted[47]. The notion that an intelligence test can somehow measure capacity or 'potential' has now been rejected[48]. There is a range of evidence supporting the contribution of environmental factors to intelligence. This includes: the observation that average IQ scores are rising[49], studies of long-term gains in intelligence[50], outcomes of successful cognitive intervention[51], instrumental enrichment studies demonstrating that intelligence is not fixed[52] and epigenetics studies showing genes being switched on and off by environmental events[53].

The important question is what teachers can do to maximize the cognitive and intellectual development of their students. One finding has been that teachers who focus on higher-order cognitive skills and questions to invite thinking are more likely to foster the intellectual development of children[54] – supporting the use of Philosophy for Children to promote the cognitive and intellectual development of students. In fact, the correlation between student's IQ scores and their rational thinking ability is weak[55]. This was illustrated by the bat and ball problem[29] – when students at Massachusetts Institute of Technology (MIT) and Harvard University made a simple reasoning error. A bat and ball cost $1.10 in total. The bat costs one dollar more than the ball. How much does the ball cost? More than 50% of students said 10 cents, rather than the correct answer of 5 cents. Ten cents would mean that the bat cost $1.10 and the total would be $1.20. IQ is no guarantee against this error. The problem is indicative of inherent cognitive bias and short cuts that can make logical reasoning our brain's second choice, not its first. It also points to the need for critical thinking.

The Challenge of Thinking

So how can we overcome inherent errors and biases in thinking? What can be done to value evidence in support of opinion? What can be done to nurture thinkers? One question that is often asked is, given the benefits of thinking independently, why there is not more emphasis on teaching thinking in schools, particularly when we know the factors[56,57] most conducive to developing these skills? Potential answers to this question include limitations in teacher professional development opportunities and high-stakes standardized assessments not requiring critical judgment. However, one reason that should not be underestimated is that thinking critically is effortful[56].

Our brains were evolved more for automatic short cuts than for higher-order thinking – the latter is slow, requires effort and comes with uncertain results. However, if students are to become habitually reasoning thinkers who can use their skills to regulate their lives, think flexibly when employed and contribute to wider society as active citizens, then an increased emphasis on philosophical thinking in the classroom would seem worthwhile. Such thinking is more likely to become the default mode when introduced at an early stage in life. This would be consistent with the finding[58] that improvements in reasoning ability resulting from Thinking Through Philosophy are sustained at least two years following the experience of philosophical inquiry.

References

1. S. Trickey and K. Topping. Collaborative philosophical enquiry for school children: Participant evaluation at 11 years. *Thinking: The Journal of Philosophy for Children*, 2007, vol. 18, issue 3, pp. 23–34.
2. D. F. Halpern. *Thought and knowledge: An introduction to critical thinking.* 1984, p. 4. Hilldale, NJ: Lawrence Erlbaum.
3. J. Bruner. *Beyond the information given.* 1974. London: George Allen & Unwin Ltd.
4. J. Dewey. *What is thought?* 1910. p. 13. Lexington, MA: D.C. Heath.
5. S. Johnson. *Teaching thinking skills. Impact No. 8.* 2001. Northampton, England: Philosophy of Education Society of Great Britain.
6. R. J. Swartz and S. Parks. *Infusing the teaching of critical and creative thinking into content instruction.* 1994. Pacific Grove, CA: Critical Thinking & Software.

7. R. Fisher. Philosophy in primary schools: Fostering thinking skills and literacy. *Reading*, July 2001, pp. 67–73. Available at: https://onlinelibrary.wiley.com/doi/abs/10.1111/1467-9345.00164 [October 20, 2018].

8. J. McPeck. Critical thinking and the trivial 'pursuit theory' of knowledge. *Teaching Philosophy*, 1984, vol. 8, issue 4, pp. 295–308.

9. R. Sutcliffe. Is teaching philosophy a high road to cognitive enhancement? *Educational and Child Psychology*, 2003, vol. 20, issue 2, pp. 65–79.

10. D. T. Willingham. Critical thinking: Why is it so hard to teach? *American Educator*, Summer 2007, pp. 8–19.

11. K. J. Topping and S. Trickey. Impact of philosophical enquiry on school students' interactive behaviour. *International Journal of Thinking Skills and Creativity*, 2007, vol. 2, pp. 73–84.

12. R. Fisher. *Teaching thinking: Philosophical enquiry in the classroom.* 1998. London: Cassell.

13. J. Haynes. Freedom and the urge to think philosophically with children. *Gifted Education International*, 2007, issue 22, pp. 229–237.

14. S. Trickey. How can students be encouraged to think critically? Infusing inquiry across subject disciplines. *Inquiry*, 2010, vol. 25, issue 3, pp. 14–21.

15. Scottish Government. *Skills for Scotland: A lifelong skills strategy.* 2007. Edinburgh, UK: Scottish Government.

16. American Management Association. *Critical skills survey.* 2012. New York, NY: American Management Association. Available at: www.amanet.org/uploaded/2012-Critical-Skills-Survey.pdf [October 20, 2018].

17. M. Korn. Bosses seek critical thinking, but what is that? *Wall Street Journal*, October 21, 2014. Available at: www.wsj.com/articles/bosses-seek-critical-thinking-but-what-is-that-1413923730 [October 25, 2018].

18. Institute for the Future. *Emerging technologies' impact on society & work in 2030: The next era of human machine partnerships.* 2017. Palo Alto, CA: Institute for the future/Dell Technologies.

19. S. Bailin and H. Siegel. Critical thinking. In N. Blake et al. (Eds.) *The Blackwell guide to the philosophy of education.* 2003, pp. 181–193. Oxford, UK: Blackwell.

20. D. S. Dunn et al. (Eds.) *Controversy in the psychology classroom: Using hot topics to foster critical thinking.* 2013. Washington DC: American Psychological Association.

21. D. F. Halpern. *Critical thinking across the curriculum: A brief edition of thought and knowledge.* 1997. Mahwah, NJ: Lawrence Erlbaum Associates.

22. R. H. Ennis. A taxonomy of critical thinking dispositions and abilities. In: J. B. Baron and R. J. Sternberg (Eds.) *Teaching thinking skills: Theory and practice.* 1987, pp. 9–26. New York. NY: WH Freeman & Co.

23. P. A. Facione. *Critical thinking: A statement of expert consensus for purposes of educational assessment and instruction (The Delphi Report).* 1990. Millbrae, CA: California Academic Press.

24. B. K. Beyer. Critical thinking: What is it? *Social Education.* 1985, vol. 49, issue 4, pp. 270–276.

25. National Governors Association (NGA) and the Council of Chief State School Officers (CCSSO). *Common core state standards initiative.* 2009. Available at: www.corestandards.org/ELA-Literacy/ W/9-10/#CCSS.ELA-Literacy.W.9-10.7 [October 23, 2018].

26. T. Van Gelder. Teaching critical thinking: Some lessons. *College Teaching,* 2005, vol. 53, issue 1, pp. 41–48.

27. M. Valverde. No terrorist attacks post 9/11 by people from countries in Trump's travel ban? *Politifact,* 2017, January 29. Available at: www.politifact.com/truth-o-meter/statements/2017/ jan/29/jerrold-nadler/have-there-been-terrorist-attacks-post-911- countri/ [October 20, 2018].

28. G. Younge. Trump fears terrorists, but more Americans are shot dead by toddlers. *The Guardian,* 2017, February 8. Available at: www.theguardian.com/commentisfree/2017/feb/08/trump-muslim- terrorists-gun-violence-america-deaths [October 25, 2018].

29. D. Kahneman. *Thinking, fast and slow.* 2011. New York, NY: Farrer, Straus & Giroux.

30. R. E. Nisbett. *Mindware: Tools for smart thinking.* 2015. New York, NY: Farrer, Straus & Giroux.

31. R. J. Sternberg. How can we teach intelligence? *Educational Leadership,* 1984, issue 42, pp. 38–48.

32. K. E. Stanovich and R. F. West. On the relative independence of thinking biases and cognitive ability. *Journal of Personality and Social Psychology,* 2008, issue 94, pp. 672–695.

33. A. Zohar, A. Degani and E. Vaaknin. Teachers' beliefs about low-achieving students and higher order thinking. *Teaching and Teacher Education*, 2001, issue 17, pp. 469–485.

34. R. W. Strong, J. R. Hanson and H. F. Silver. *Questioning styles & strategies: Manual #3*. 1980. Woodbridge, NJ: The Thoughtful Education Press.

35. J. E. Ormrod. *Essentials of educational psychology (Third Edition) Instructors online manual*. 2009. Upper Saddle River, NJ: Pearson.

36. M. Lipman. *Harry Stottlemeier's discovery*. 1974. Montclair, NJ: Institute for the Advancement of Philosophy for Children (IAPC).

37. A. Kohn. *Feel-bad education: And other contrarian essays on children and schooling*. 2011. Boston, MA: Beacon Press.

38. R. Sutcliffe. Constructive thinking and reconstructive thinking: Some thought about de Bono's thoughts. *If...Then: The Journal of Philosophical Enquiry in Education*, 1977, issue 3, June 3.

39. L. Carroll. *Through the looking-glass*. 1871. Basingstoke, UK: MacMillan. Available at: www.gutenberg.org/files/12/12-h/12-h.htm#link2HCH0004 [October 21, 2018].

40. UNESCO. *Philosophy: A school of freedom*. 2007. Paris, France: UNESCO. Available at: http://unesdoc.unesco.org/images/0015/001541/154173e.pdf [October 25, 2018].

41. R. Fisher. *Teaching children to think*. 1995. Kingston-upon Thames, England: Stanley Thornes.

42. H. J. Eysenck and L. Kamin. *Intelligence: The battle for the mind*. 1981. London: Pan Books.

43. C. Burt. *Mental and scholastic tests (2nd Edition)*. 1947. London: Staples.

44. A. Jensen. How much can we boost IQ and scholastic achievement? *Harvard Educational Review*, 1969, vol. 39, issue 1, pp. 1–123.

45. R. J. Hernstein and C. Murray. *The Bell Curve: Intelligence and class structure in American life*. 1994. New York, NY: Free Press.

46. L. S. Hearnshaw. *Cyril Burt: Psychologist*. 1979. Ithaca, NY: Cornell University Press.

47. H. Gardner. Cracking open the IQ box. In: S. Fraser (Ed.) *The bell curve wars: Race, intelligence, and the future of America*. 1995, pp. 23–35. New York. NY: Basic Books.

48. Blogs.scientificamerican.com. What Do IQ Tests Test? Interview with psychologist W. Joel Schneider. *Beautiful Minds, Scientific American Blog Network*, 2014, February 3. Available

at: http://blogs.scientificamerican.com/beautiful-minds/2014/02/ 03/what-do-iq-tests-test-interview-with-psychologist-w-joel-schneider/ [October 26, 2018].

49. J. R. Flynn. Requiem for nutrition as the cause of IQ gains: Raven's gains in Britain 1938–2008. *Economics and Human Biology,* 2009, vol. 7, issue 1, pp. 18–27.

50. U. Neisser (Ed.) *The rising curve: Long term gains in IQ and related measures.* 1998. Washington DC: American Psychological Association.

51. F. A. Campbell and C. T. Ramey. Effects of early intervention on intellectual and academic achievement: A follow-up study of children from low-income families. *Child Development,* 1994, issue 65, pp. 684–698.

52. R. Feuerstein. The theory of structural cognitive modifiability. In: B. Presseisen (Ed.). *Learning and thinking styles: Classroom interaction.* Washington DC: National Education Association, 1990, pp. 68–134.

53. B. Lipton. *The biology of belief.* 2005. Carlsbad, CA: Hay House Inc.

54. R. J. Sternberg and L. S. Swerling. *Teaching for thinking.* 1996. Washington DC: American Psychological Association.

55. K. E. Stanovich and R. F. West. What intelligence tests miss. *The Psychologist,* 2014, vol. 27, issue 2, pp. 80–83.

56. P. C. Abrami et al. Instructional interventions affecting critical thinking skills and dispositions: A stage 1 meta-analysis. *Review of Educational Research,* 2008, vol. 78, issue 4.

57. T. Van Gelder. Teaching critical thinking: Some lessons. *College Teaching,* 2005, vol. 53, issue 1, pp. 41–48.

58. K. J. Topping and S. Trickey. Collaborative philosophical enquiry for school children: Cognitive gains at two-year follow-up. *British Journal of Educational Psychology,* 2007, issue 77, pp. 781–796.

7

Communication, Dialogue and Social/Emotional Development

When asked after participation what they thought the wider effects of Philosophy for Children were, Peter (aged 10) noted: 'I think people are able to speak out more than they used to.' Mary (also aged 10) had a wider view: 'There is more peace in the school and everyone learns to like one another.' It has been suggested in this book that intrinsic motivation (motivation from within) is conducive to 'deep learning' that can be applied outside the classroom to real-world issues. The scope for intrinsic motivation to develop is increased when students' basic psychological needs are met in the classroom. These include students' need for connection with other students. Students are, after all, social creatures. 'No man is an island'[1]. Schools that emphasize students' need for belonging to a school community get better academic results[2]. The effective school sees itself not just as a teaching institution but also as a caring learning community.

Philosophical inquiry aims to gradually develop a respectful community of inquiry consistent with this concept. Such communities encourage students to become more confident in their ability to communicate their views with others in the classroom[3]. This chapter will look at what helps to make this possible. Consideration will be given to the contribution that Thinking Through Philosophy makes to a student's social and emotional development. While this is important in its own right, enhanced social and emotional behaviors also impact academic success in school and ultimately success in life[4]. Improving communication in the classroom is seen as an important prerequisite. This chapter will analyze factors conducive to communication with a view to how philosophical inquiry can best be implemented, thereby supporting social development as well as cognitive development.

Thought and Feeling Are Inseparable

Thinking Through Philosophy aims to help students become more independent thinkers. In reality, thought and feeling are inseparable, a view supported by medical, psychological and philosophical perspectives. How we think and what we think about will have a direct bearing on our emotional state. The degree to which individuals integrate their emotional and rational responses shapes their ability to make good judgments and influences emotional well-being. Emotion is part of cognition and feelings are a powerful influence on reasoning.[5] The medical view that thought and feeling are inseparable resonates with psychological perspectives about thinking[6] and also with philosophical perspectives.[7]

The medical perspective associates the brain's prefrontal cortex with reasoning, planning and other higher-order thinking processes. This part of the brain has evolved more recently compared to areas associated with more primitive responses like automatic flight and flight reactions. The latter, well-established survival system is likely to dominate more recently evolved higher-order thinking systems when the need arises. Higher-order thinking is associated with effortful 'System 2 thinking'[6] that potentially moderates the impulsivity and helps self-regulation of 'System 1 thinking'. Self-regulation is our ability to manage our own behavior and emotional reactions that would otherwise obstruct goal attainment. This is important to teachers, as self-regulating students set more ambitious academic goals and achieve at higher levels in the classroom.[8]

However, System 1 thinking seems more powerful than the intentional, reasoned thinking in System 2. Intentional thinking is more effortful and tiring than System 1 thinking, which requires no conscious effort and provides mental short cuts. These latter heuristics usually lead to good decisions, but can be prone to predictable and systematic errors. The relationship of System 1 to System 2 thinking has been likened to a little rider (System 2) on top of a huge elephant of emotions and intuitions (System 1)[9]. The elephant is slow to turn and liable to stampede at threats. The higher cognitive processes aimed for in philosophical inquiry parallel the little rider. They can guide behavior and thinking but require conscious effort. Critical thinking is not the standard default mode for most people.

This metaphor has implications for teachers leading inquiries. An important goal of education should be self-regulation to improve the management of impulsivity and distractibility. In developing this process, teachers continually model behaviors both consciously and unconsciously. Their emotions are contagious. They can help or hinder self-regulation. Learning to moderate impulsive reactions is not easy. Aristotle wrote over 2000 years ago in *The Art of Rhetoric*[10]: 'anybody can become angry, that is easy; but to be angry with the right person, and to the right degree, and at the right time, and for the right purpose, and in the right way, that is not within everybody's power, that is not easy'.

A more modern version of Aristotle's thinking can be found in the concept of emotional intelligence. Emotional intelligence has been defined[11] as the ability to recognize our own emotions and those of others, to motivate ourselves and to manage emotions well in ourselves and in our relationships. Aristotle's statement appreciates the 'hard-wiring' of our brains to react instantly to threat rather than to respond thoughtfully. The survival of the human race has been dependent on this fight/flight capacity.

However, modern threats are likely to be less of an immediate danger to life. Fighting and fleeing are rarely the most productive way of managing psychological threat. Psychological threat in the classroom is more likely to be about threat to self-esteem. Building communication skills and confidence in the classroom is more effective in raising the threshold for inappropriate impulsivity to occur. This chapter will consider the contribution of philosophical inquiry to self-management and social well-being.

It is worth drawing attention to the Stanford marshmallow experiment to demonstrate the educational value of self-regulation and reduction in impulsivity.[12] In the marshmallow study, four-year old children who were given a marshmallow were told that the adult had to leave the room briefly. If the child could wait for the adult to return without eating their marshmallow, they were told they would receive an extra one. Some participants waited for an endless 15–20 minutes for the adult to return, while others consumed their marshmallow within seconds. The significance of the experiment became apparent when the children were followed up at aged 16+ years. Those who had inhibited their impulse to consume the marshmallow were found to be more socially competent, better able to cope with frustration, better able to reason and achieved significantly higher SAT test scores. The ability to self-regulate and moderate excessive impulsivity appears a worthy goal for educators and merits consideration of ways in which this might be achieved.

Can Philosophical Inquiry Help Re-Educate Emotions?

Philosophy for Children is a communal, reasoned search for truth within a supportive, respectful group. This is complicated by inherent thinking biases and the relative weakness of System 2 thinking. This makes people vulnerable to false information. There is an automatic instinct to believe stories that correspond to existing beliefs. As some politicians have realized, reasoned argument can be less successful than a simple appeal to emotional prejudice.

While higher-order thinking is not the automatic default response for most, aspects of higher-order thinking can be strengthened through regular practice of philosophical inquiry[13]. Philosophy for Children supports social development[14] as well as autonomous thinking. Matthew Lipman's colleague, Ann Sharp, emphasized[7] the fusion of thinking and feeling in caring thinking and argued for the need to educate emotions in order to make good judgments. She suggested that each emotion entails a cognitive appraisal, for example, to be angry is to make a judgment that one has been wronged. Uncovering an underlying belief behind emotions and submitting that belief to inquiry is a way of discovering that the belief lacks any validity. Such a process helps to educate emotions and shifts the balance between System 1 and System 2 thinking.

Many System 1 behaviors are learned. Some are reasonable and some are not reasonable. There is no standard response for any particular incident – we each respond individually and our responses have been molded by many different factors. If you deal with a boy about a playground misdemeanor his response might be 'Yes, but I've got a temper', as if that was a reasonable cause. Philosophical inquiry helps highlight your own behavior and that of others and enables you to see the causes of individual intuitive responses. Armed with that knowledge, the individual can better choose a more appropriate response. (This could, of course, be to show some anger, but coming from a different cause – and is more likely to be measured and appropriate). All this reinforces the importance of a class having dialogues on questions from a range of themes involving emotional issues. In this way a range of responses around 'emotional' questions are consciously examined and evaluated in a safe environment. When the students are later involved in a life situation the knowledge gained from the dialogue acts to enable a brief 'pause' – just enough to choose an appropriate behavior! This helps a student move towards making conscious decisions about particular responses rather than just act mechanically and habitually. ('I've got a temper. I acted that way last time in response to a similar situation and I'll act that way next time.') Of course, things don't change instantly, but over time a shift is evident, both to the student and to the observer.

Parallels Between Philosophical Inquiry and 'Cognitive Behavioral Therapy'

Support for the value of challenging counterproductive beliefs comes from cognitive behavioral therapy (CBT)[15], reflecting the link between what people think and how they feel. There are parallels in the processes of CBT and Philosophy for Children. CBT focuses on how people respond to their interpretations of experiences and encourages the monitoring of thoughts. Clients are encouraged to consider the evidence supporting those thoughts. Beliefs are subjected to critical evaluation. The willingness to change one's mind in the light of evidence and collaborative dialogue (as in philosophical inquiry) lead to changes in feelings. In CBT children are encouraged to think like a judge in court in relation to the evidence supporting their own thought processes[16]. The therapist uses Socratic questions to encourage changes in thinking to improve emotional well-being.

In view of these parallels, it is not surprising that philosophical inquiry helps children recognize their emotions and increases the likelihood of benefit from cognitive behavioral therapy[17]. It was also not surprising that social emotional gains were found in the Scottish evaluation of the Thinking Through Philosophy program[18,19]. The Scottish study provided evidence from pupil questionnaires and standardized tests that collaborative inquiry led to improvements in communication skills, confidence, concentration and self-esteem. Anecdotal observations also suggested that the collaborative process helped students self-regulate feelings and reduce impulsivity, leading to improvements in behavior and relationships. Communication skills, listening and participation would appear key elements in promoting student social and emotional well-being. Philosophical inquiry requires being listened to, belonging to a participative community and developing a connection with others. The sharing of feelings, experiences, perspectives and ideas in communities of inquiry is conducive to affective as well as cognitive development[20].

Participation, Communication and Social Well-being

A strong school culture of participation and collaboration supports the learning of communication and collaboration skills and leads to enhanced self-esteem and a greater sense of self-efficacy[21]. Participation is a key factor in promoting the emotional well-being of school-age children and in the morale and performance of both teachers and students[22]. Participation has been found to increase following regular collaborative inquiry[23]. Developing communication skills is a vital part of feeling good about oneself and relating effectively to others. Communication is also the basis of relationships and listening is a central skill in communication. The undivided, unconditional attention of other students is likely to promote positive feelings in a student expressing their opinion. Such attention makes students feel interesting, worthwhile and understood. This is relevant to philosophical inquiry, where the elements of listening, communication and participation are central.

Communication in the Classroom

Discussion with peers can enhance learning[24]. When students express their ideas in class, they must organize and process their thoughts. They may discover gaps in their understanding and encounter explanations better than their own. Well-structured, thoughtful discussion with peers can construct meaning to provide a more effective learning experience for all. However, the prevalence of discussion may be overestimated and much discussion that does take place may be of dubious effectiveness[25]. The proportion of time that teachers talk in classroom versus the time students talk does not seem to have shifted dramatically since a study in the 1960s[26] found teachers doing 70% of the talking (as against their students' 30%) in the classroom. Forty years after this early study, the current authors still found teachers talking 59% of the time in a baseline assessment prior to involvement in Thinking through Philosophy[24].

In addition, research studies[27] have found:

◆ A relative scarcity of teacher talk that really challenges pupils to think for themselves

◆ A low level of cognitive demand in many classroom questions

◆ The continued prevalence of closed questions

◆ The rarity of autonomous pupil discussion and problem-solving.

In contrast, when oral and collaborative activities are well structured, they maintain children's time on task more consistently than solitary written tasks[28].

Dialogue in Thinking Through Philosophy is both well structured and collaborative and can shift the balance of classroom interaction from 59% teacher talk to 44% after six months[23]. It seems reasonable to speculate that increased student participation in class would further increase over a longer period of time. However, the quantity of student talk is a lesser objective than improving the quality of dialogue taking place. Several factors contribute to the quality of communication and dialogue and these will be considered during the remainder of this chapter.

Improving Communication and Dialogue in the Classroom

Observations of classroom talk have indicated a lack of student input and questions. For example,[29] in one hour, teachers were found to ask eighty-four questions, while all the pupils combined only asked two questions. Students may be reluctant to ask questions in case they display ignorance, thus risking embarrassment. They may also have concerns about disrupting the lesson when the teacher is trying to get though a lot of material.

Such findings suggest an underestimation of the value of student questions – as espoused by Socrates in ancient Greece. Socratic dialogue contrasts with the predominant teacher/student interaction that consists of rapid teacher questions requiring factual answers. This allows little room for student questions or meaningful debate. Socrates advised that children should devote themselves to the techniques of asking as well as answering questions, in contrast to contemporary practice that disproportionately values answers over questions. When teachers value student questions and resultant discussion, they are not only teaching for understanding but also enhancing communication and social development.

When teachers ask questions, there can be as many as 100 questions per hour and 80% of these can require simple recall[30]. Closed teacher questions are primarily designed to test memory but have the disadvantage of preventing discussion. In this 'recitation' pattern of classroom interaction, teachers do most of the cognitive work and rarely ask students to elaborate their answers. The teacher is the 'sage on the stage' rather than the 'guide by your side'. Recitation patterns are typified by teacher led 'IRF' exchanges[31] consisting of the teacher *Initiating* a question, a student *Response* to the question and the teacher *Feedback* (evaluation) and then the next question. These patterns breed passive, uncritical students and stop discussion. This is the opposite to what is sought in Philosophy for Children. Research in U. S. schools has traditionally shown that classroom discourse has been 'overwhelmingly monologic', being dominated by teacher talk. Only a small minority of teachers ask authentic questions (without pre-specified answers) and follow up student responses[31]. Recitation continues to be the predominant pattern of teacher-student communication in American and British classrooms[32,33].

Over the years such a recitation pattern can lead to a decline in curiosity as the student works his or her way through the educational system. This reminds us of Matthew Lipman's quote[34] at the start of the first chapter about young children initially bringing curiosity and imagination when entering the educational system. The recitation pattern is understandable given the teacher's need to cover the voluminous curriculum. It has also been suggested that recitation patterns have dominated because of the lack of professional development opportunities to support teachers in interacting differently[35]. A more open style of dialogue can also seem risky for teachers in terms of control and discipline. Students may be less comfortable with participating in dialogue if they are not used to thinking for themselves or lack necessary social skills. They might also be reluctant to ask questions to avoid mistakes that might threaten their self-worth.

Evidence of a lack of 'good talk' in classrooms is linked to a faulty assumption that children inherently know how to discuss[36]. Philosophy for Children provides a practical process for teachers to structure classroom discussion. Students are likely to learn from each other during this process. For example, a student might hear another asking for evidence and (through modeling) be more likely to internalize this behavior and do the same. Real discussion best takes place when the questions perplex the teacher as well as the students.[37] If the questions chosen for discussion are perplexing for all participants, including the teacher, then communication is likely to become more interactive and more meaningful. This is where philosophical inquiry comes into its own, as philosophical concepts such as 'love' and 'fairness' lack simple definition and are therefore rich in 'puzzlement' and ambiguity.

Classroom dialogue not only rests on open-ended questions but on the emotional climate created by the teacher. That climate is evident in the teacher's willingness to listen respectfully to what students have to say and follow up. A community of inquiry approach also encourages students to respect each other, to listen and to take each other's ideas seriously. The teacher's higher-order questions include elements likely to sustain communication and engagement with students and encourage social development.

Students need fewer and better questions that focus on ideas rather than facts[38]. Practical examples of open-ended, authentic questions that open up dialogue were provided in Chapter 3. Such questions are likely to facilitate classroom discussion by allowing more flexibility and increased depth of discussion[39]. They can also encourage co-operation between students and help establish rapport. The effectiveness of open-ended questioning in prompting social development as well as intellectual development has been demonstrated even in pre-school education[40]. In addition to open-ended teacher questions, the Think/Pair/Share strategy (Chapter 3) and students being motivated by their own questions, two other practical strategies are described below. These are likely to have contributed to increased participation in Philosophy for Children[14,23].

The first of these expands upon the concept of thinking time (Chapter 3). This is a relatively simple way of increasing the likelihood that students will think more carefully about whatever question is being raised. This idea is based on the finding[41] that when teachers ask a question, they typically wait one second or less for the student's response. If this is not forthcoming, the teacher tends to ask another student the same question, rephrases the original question or answers the question themselves. This suggests that teachers can be reluctant to let much time elapse following questioning.

However, when teachers allow at least three seconds to elapse after their own questions and after student comments, more students participate, students begin to respond to one another's questions and comments, students are more likely to support their reasoning with evidence or logic and more likely to speculate when they do not know the answer. Learning increases. When teachers pause for three seconds, they also ask fewer questions requiring mere recall of facts, ask more thought-provoking questions, modify discussion to accommodate student's comments and questions and allow classes to pursue a topic in greater depth[42].

When answering a question that requires only recall, usually the response can be immediate if the answer is known. A question related to a complex philosophical concept requires an answer to be formulated that is likely to be new and original. To allow this to emerge a little time is necessary. Students should also be encouraged to speak when the germ of an idea shows itself – the teacher should allow the response to be formulated as he or she listens carefully to what the student is saying. It is not always necessary to completely formulate a response in mind before starting to speak. This is very much a higher-order of thinking and should be encouraged. Of course, sometimes as the thread of thought unravels the speaker may see that it is going nowhere or is incomplete and may stop speaking. This is absolutely acceptable. When maintaining eye contact and showing interest, silence can be an invitation to develop a thought and say more.[43] This is particularly relevant to teachers leading philosophical inquiry, when it is crucial that students feel listened to and understood and are sufficiently comfortable to engage. Thinking cannot be separated from the social and emotional aspects of discussion.

The second strategy is 'contingent follow-ups'[44] that help facilitate inquiry. In the IRF pattern, if the teacher recasts the Feedback move as a 'Follow-up' move, the exchange can be extended into a more conversation-like discourse. If the teacher's follow-up builds on a student's contribution, the teacher is validating that contribution and extending student thinking. The third move has the power to encourage further conversation or shut down exchanges. It is imperative that the teacher communicates a genuine interest in the thinking behind the student's response.

One way to follow up the student's initial response is through the use of open or authentic questions to seek clarification and probe reasons and evidence (as in examples given in Chapter 3). Another follow-up response would be to simply withhold evaluative judgment by a statement such as 'that's interesting', 'Ah-ha' or 'I see' – followed up with 'Can you tell us a little more?' The teacher can respond in ways that benefit the whole group by repeating what the student has said for emphasis or by elaborating by explaining the significance of the student's remark. It is important that the teacher provides opportunities to 'think in the moment' through follow-up questions that are contingent on what the student has just said[45]. The teacher also serves as a model so that, in the longer term, students take on the teacher role of questioning to shape the talk of their peers. Genuine dialogical teaching is likely to take time, particularly with younger students who are used to classroom interactions going through the teacher.

Summary

The process of philosophical inquiry encourages social and emotional learning. This is not only a goal in its own right but also can contribute to wider academic success. For interactive thinking communities to promote social and intellectual development, consideration has to be given to the way teachers use questions and follow up student comments. Evaluations of philosophical inquiry have provided evidence that communities of inquiry can contribute to positive social and emotional outcomes. This chapter has considered strategies that teachers can use in philosophical inquiry to reduce impulsivity, sustain communication and increase participation thereby promoting student well-being in the classroom. However, the beauty of philosophical inquiry is that when well done, the teacher does not have to ensure painstakingly that each of the aspects or points mentioned above are covered – this naturally takes place through the flow of the process.

References

1. J. Donne. *Devotions upon emergent occasions*, Meditation XVII. 1624. Available at: http://www.gutenberg.org/files/23772/23772-h/23772-h.htm

2. E. Schaps, Creating a school community. *Educational Leadership*, 2003, vol. 60, issue 6, pp. 31–33.

3. S. Trickey and K. J. Topping. Collaborative philosophical enquiry for school children: Participant evaluation at 11 years. *Thinking: The Journal of Philosophy for Children*, 2007, vol. 18, issue 3, pp. 23–34.

4. J. E. Zins, R. P. Weissberg, M. C. Wang and H. J. Walberg (Eds.). *Building academic success on social and emotional learning: What does the research say?* 2004, New York, NY: Teachers College, Columbia University.

5. A. R. Damasio, *Descartes' error: Emotion, reason and the human brain:* 1994. New York, NY: G. P. Putnam's Sons.

6. D. Kahneman, *Thinking, fast and slow.* 2011. New York, NY: Farrer, Straus & Giroux.

7. A. M. Sharp. Education of the emotions in the classroom community of inquiry. *Gifted Children International.* 2007, vol. 22, pp. 248–257.

8. J. E. Ormrod. *Essentials of educational psychology (Third Edition).* 2009. Upper Saddle River, NJ: Pearson.

9. G. Tsipursky and L. Holliday. *The truth-seeker's handbook: A science-based guide.* 2017. Columbus, OH: Intentional Insights Press.

10. W. D. Ross (Ed.) *Ars Rhetorica.* 1959. Oxford: Oxford University Press.

11. P. Salovey and J. D. Mayer. Emotional intelligence. *Imagination, Cognition, and Personality,* 1990, vol. 9, pp. 185–211.

12. W. Y. Mischel, Y. Shoda and M. L. Rodriguez. Delay of gratification in children. *Science,* 1989, vol. 244, pp. 933–938.

13. K. J. Topping and S. Trickey, Collaborative philosophical enquiry for school children: Cognitive effects at 10–12 years. *British Journal of Educational Psychology,* 2007, vol. 77, pp. 271–288.

14. N. Siddiqui, S. Gorard and B. H. See. *Non-cognitive impacts of Philosophy for Children, Project report.* 2017. Durham, England: School of Education, Durham University.

15. A. T. Beck, Cognitive therapy: Nature and relation to behavior therapy. *Behavior Therapy,* 1970, vol. 1, issue 2, pp. 141–284.

16. C. Creswell and L. Willets. *Overcoming your child's fears and worries.* 2007, London: Constable & Robinson.

17. E. Doherr. *The demonstration of cognitive abilities central to cognitive behavioural therapy in young people: Examining the influence of age and teaching method on degree of ability.* 2000, Unpublished clinical psychology doctoral dissertation, University of East Anglia.

18. S. Trickey and K. J. Topping. Collaborative philosophical enquiry for school children: Participant evaluation at 11 years. *Thinking: The Journal of Philosophy for Children,* 2007, vol. 18, issue 3, pp. 23–34.

19. S. Trickey & K. J. Topping. Collaborative philosophical enquiry for school children: socio-emotional effects at 11–12 years. *School Psychology International,* 2006, vol. 27, issue 5, pp. 599–614.

20. Department for Education and Skills. *Excellence and enjoyment: Social and emotional aspects of learning.* 2005. p. 56. London: Department for Education and Skills.

21. Mentality. *Mental health improvement: What works? A briefing developed by Mentality for the Scottish Executive.* 2002. Edinburgh: Scottish Executive.

22. K. Weare. *Promoting mental, emotional and social health.* 2002. New York: Routledge.

23. K. J. Topping and S. Trickey. Impact of philosophical enquiry on school students' interactive behaviour. *International Journal of Thinking Skills and Creativity,* 2007, vol. 2, pp. 73–84.

24. J. E. Ormrod. *Essentials of educational psychology (Third Edition).* 2009. p. 300. Upper Saddle River, NJ: Pearson.

25. N. Mercer. *Word and minds: How we use language to think together.* 2000. London: Routledge.

26. N. Flanders. *The language of the classroom. Cooperative Research Project #1497.* 1963, Institute of Psychological Research, Columbia University.

27. R. Alexander. *Towards dialogic teaching.* 2004. Cambridge, England: Dialogos.

28. R. Alexander. *Versions of primary education.* 1995. London: Routledge.

29. J. T. Dillon. *The practice of questioning.* 1990. London: Routledge.

30. M. Nystrand, et al., *Opening dialogue: Understanding the dynamics of language and learning in the English classroom.* 1997. New York: Teachers College Press.

31. M. Coulthard (Ed). *Advances in spoken discourse analysis.* 1992. London: Routledge.

32. J. A. Walsh and B. D. Satter. *Questioning for classroom discussion: purposeful speaking, engaged listening, deep thinking.* 2015. p. 14. Alexandria, VA: ASCD.

33. M. G. McKeown and I. L. Beck. Effective talk is reading comprehension instruction. In L. B. Resnick, C. S. C. Asterhan and S. N. Clarke (Eds.) *Socializing intelligence though academic talk and dialogue.* 2015. p. 52. Washington DC: American Education Research Association.

34. M. Lipman, A. M. Sharp and F. Oscanyon. *Philosophy in the classroom.* 1980. Philadelphia, PA: Temple University Press

35. R. Tharp and R. Gallimore. *Rousing minds to life: Teaching, learning and schooling in social context.* 1988. Cambridge: Cambridge University Press.

36. L. Dawes, N. Mercer and R. Wegerif. *Thinking together: A programme of activities for developing speaking, listening and thinking skills for children aged 8–11.* 2000. Cambridge: Cambridge University Press.

37. J. T. Dillon. *Questioning and teaching.* 1988. London: Routledge.

38. R. Fisher. *Teaching children to think.* 2005. Cheltenham: Nelson Thorne.

39. L. Cohen and L. Manion. *Research methods in education.* 1980. London: Routledge.

40. K. Sylva, et al. *The effective provision of pre-school education (EPPI) Project.* 2003. London: University of London.

41. M. B. Rowe. Wait time and rewards as instructional variables, their influence on language, logic and fate control. *Journal of Research in Science Teaching,* 1974, vol. 11, issue 2, pp. 81–84.

42. M. B. Rowe. (1986) Wait time: Slowing down may be a way of speeding up! *Journal of Teacher Education,* 1986; vol. 37, pp. 43–50.

43. R.W. Strong, J. R. Hanson and H. F. Silver. *Questioning styles & strategies: Manual #3 in the unity in diversity series.* 1980. Woodbridge, New Jersey: The Thoughtful Education Press.

44. G. Wells. Re-evaluating the IRF sequence: A proposal for the articulation of theories of activity and discourse for the analysis of teaching and learning in the classroom. 1993. *Linguistics and Education,* vol. 5, pp. 1–37.

45. M. P. Boyd and L. Galda. *Real talk in elementary classrooms: Effective oral language practice.* 2011. The Guilford Press: New York.

8

Does P4C Work? Evaluation Research

In their classic 1980 book, Lipman, Sharp and Oscanyon said: 'It has been argued…that humanistic studies should not be compelled to justify themselves by virtue of empirical evidence that they promote academic improvement…But this argument is not likely to be persuasive to the vast majority of school administrators…If philosophy is to be admitted into the curriculum, it will succeed in doing so only if it can demonstrate to those who run the schools that it can make a significant difference in the child's overall performance'[1] (p. 44). Matthew Lipman fully appreciated the need to evaluate education programs if they are to be taken seriously. This chapter poses the question 'Does P4C work?' It will interest those who seek evidence. It is important that in an era of ever-changing educational fads and fashions, practitioners are confident that philosophical inquiry has a sound evidence base. Although far from a simple panacea, P4C has proven durable since Lipman's first publications in the early 1970s. This chapter will include the current authors' findings from an evaluative four-year longitudinal study, together with a wider summary of other evaluation findings relating to P4C.

Why Evaluate the Effectiveness of Thinking Programs?

One reason why we need to evaluate programs is that assumptions that education programs work have frequently proved to be wrong. Such assumptions have led to considerable time and money being invested in ineffective programs such as the Head Start (preschool intervention) programs, Critical Incident Stress Debriefing and the Scared Straight program for adolescents at risk of criminal behavior. In all of these instances, alternative approaches had been evaluated that could have worked better. For example, the $200 billion invested in Head Start would have been better spent on providing more intensive experiences to a smaller number of particularly vulnerable children.[2] While the authors suspect that it is most unlikely that such sums will be invested in Philosophy for Children, it nevertheless remains important that the inquiry process has been subjected to careful and thorough evaluation.

It is also important that research be sound. Some research sounds impressive but can be misleading. For example, research on the effect of average class size on academic performance based on multiple regression analysis (MRA) can give one impression about causality while randomized control experiments give another. Studies that randomly assign subjects to treatment or control groups are superior to MRA-based research, as the latter is prone to errors based on self-selection[2]. This chapter will therefore primarily focus on controlled research studies, that is, where a group of students experiencing philosophical inquiry is matched by a group who have not had such an experience.

Placing Philosophy for Children within Thinking Skills Interventions

Philosophy for Children aims to promote critical and creative thinking and is an example of a thinking skills program. The term thinking skills can be thought (wrongly) to imply skills that are easily 'trainable'. However, cultivating thinking habits and dispositions takes time, teacher commitment and active student engagement. One way of investigating the question of whether thinking skills programs have a measurable effect has been through meta-analyses – studies that synthesize the results of many different evaluation studies into a single quantitative index of effectiveness ('effect size', or ES). Meta-analysis studies measure and combine ESs to indicate the magnitude of the difference between groups that underwent a thinking intervention and control groups that had not. ESs range from over 1.00 (indicating a large positive effect) through 0 (no effect) to over −1 (strong negative effect).

One such study concluded that thinking skills programs were effective in improving pupils' performance on a range of tested outcomes[3]. This study obtained an overall mean ES of 0.62 on standardized cognitive tests, an impact described as high[4]. This effect would move a class ranked at 50th place in a league table of 100 similar classes to 26th place, a percentile gain of 24 points. Not every meta-analysis has obtained such a high effect. For example, another meta-analysis of the effects of critical thinking programs that used studies of more variable quality obtained an ES of 0.34.[5] Meta-analyses of evaluations of single cognitive intervention programs tend to yield a moderate positive ES. For example, for Feuerstein's instrumental enrichment (FIE) an ES of 0.43 on reasoning ability was found[6]. The effect of Philosophy for Children seems similar to that for FIE and is discussed in more detail later in this chapter.

The majority of evaluation studies on thinking skills interventions, including Philosophy for Children, have reported a positive impact across measures such as reasoning and attainment. The behavior of the teacher has been cited as a crucial variable necessary for establishing collaborative group work and effective patterns of talk and in eliciting student responses. One interesting finding is that the impact of thinking programs can increase over time. This has been reported with both FIE[7] and the Cognitive Acceleration of Science (CASE) programs[8]. In the former instance, gains from FIE program were not only maintained but also increased two years following the completion of the original program. In the instance of CASE, there was some immediate improvement, but the most striking effects were shown three years later when students took national examinations or tests. These gains were not only evident in science (where there was an average gain of the order of one grade) but also transferred to math and English. The CASE results have been replicated in United States[9].

Concerns have been expressed[10] about the transferability and sustainability of gains from thinking skills program to other contexts, as with any intervention program. Programs that have been found to have a measurable positive impact (such as CASE, FIE and Thinking Through Philosophy[11]) include 'bridging' exercises to support transfer of thinking to other contexts. The results of follow-up evaluations for these programs suggest that under some circumstances gains from thinking skills interventions can be both sustainable and transferable.

Another theme that has emerged from evaluations of successful cognitive interventions is their strong focus on teacher development. For thinking skills programs to work, teachers need support from credible trainers and opportunities to reflect on their practice while engaged in action[12]. Quality professional development must be sustained over time and be non-threatening and collaborative in nature. Professional development should feel owned by the teacher and involve practical formative feedback[13]. Professional development should also be about providing opportunities for teachers to reflect on their practice so they come up with their own suggestions to improve the effectiveness of what they are doing. This is in stark contrast to the notion of an expert 'parachuting' in for a training session, never to be seen again[14].

Sternberg and Bhana[15] view Philosophy for Children as highly teacher-sensitive and requiring extensive teacher training. Sternberg suggested that the success of the P4C program depends on the teacher as much as the materials and could work outstandingly well with a gifted teacher. While a full examination of professional development issues is beyond the scope of this chapter, positive outcomes from Philosophy for Children will inevitably be dependent on the quality of training available to teachers. The Thinking Through Philosophy initiative involved the secondment of one of the current authors (a school principal at the time) together with part-time secondment of two experienced senior teachers. This group provided credible guidance and support to colleagues who had varied experience and skills for the duration of the project. Class groups varied in academic ability and socioeconomic grouping but the teachers also varied and were very much a mixed group in terms of ability and experience. There were several first-year teachers and others in their first five years as well as some skilled teachers, yet all class groups showed gains across the different measurements – although these gains differed from teacher to teacher.

Early Evaluative Studies of Philosophy for Children

The earliest studies came from Lipman, who reported a positive impact of Philosophy for Children on reasoning ability, reading and mathematics in a series of controlled experiments in the 1970s[1]. A body of research followed, reporting consistent gains in cognitive skills[16,17,18]. An extensive list of such studies is available on the website of the Institute for the Advancement of Philosophy for Children[19]. Reasoning was measured by standardized tests such as the New Jersey Test of Reasoning Skills, Cornell Critical Thinking Test, Whimbey Analytical Skills Inventory and the Cognitive Abilities Test[20]. A wide range of critical thinking skills were assessed in these tests. For example, Shipman's New Jersey Test of Reasoning Skills analyzed 22 reasoning skills including analogical reasoning, avoiding jumping to conclusions, inductive reasoning, identifying good reasons and detecting underlying assumptions. A more recent example of a critical thinking test would be the Halpern Critical Thinking Assessment (HCTA)[21], that also claims to predict real-world outcomes of critical thinking.

By 1996, concerns were being voiced over the quality of some evaluations of Philosophy for Children, particularly the lack of adequate control groups. Sternberg and Bhana[15] reviewed 20 evaluation studies of P4C and found issues around subject dropout, subject selection, durability, transfer and subject population. Experimenter bias had not generally been addressed and statistical analysis was often reported in minimal detail. Despite these methodological concerns, the authors were nevertheless favorably disposed toward Philosophy for Children, noting widespread gains on tests of critical thinking. They also believed that Philosophy for Children was more motivating than most thinking skills training programs and more likely to teach durable and transferrable thinking skills than any other program[22].

Systematic Reviews of Philosophy for Children

Two meta-analyses in 2004[23] and 2005[24] sought to address some of the issues identified by Sternberg and Bhana through systematic reviews of selected studies. These systematic reviews were based on studies that had used pre–post measurement of experimental and control groups and in that sense followed the best-evidence tradition.[25] In the first review, the authors located a total of ten controlled studies to establish causal relationships. A number of studies were rejected for lacking a control group or sufficient data necessary to calculate an ES. An overall ES of 0.42 provided evidence of a moderate positive effect in the use of Philosophy for Children in different countries. This was closely followed by a second meta-analysis[24] that selected eighteen studies for inclusion. The average ES was 0.58 but with considerable variance between different studies.

The cognitive outcomes referred to so far have all been from quantitative research. However, some researchers[26] have advocated a more qualitative approach to assessing thinking outcomes. Qualitative approaches access the perceptions of the participants rather than relying solely on gathering observable empirical data. The current authors used both quantitative and qualitative methods to evaluate the Thinking Through Philosophy program and triangulated overlapping and related outcomes to increase the reliability of their findings.

Evaluating the Thinking Through Philosophy Program

The Thinking Through Philosophy study investigated outcomes arising from the regular use of collaborative philosophical inquiry in elementary school classrooms with students approximately ten years of age. The context can be described as 'ecologically valid' in that the project took place with ordinary mixed-ability classes of approximately 25 students. This contrasts with studies that had assessed small group work with selected high ability students. The inquiries were facilitated by teachers with limited previous experience of such methods.

The evaluation used three methods encompassing both quantitative and qualitative perspectives. Standardized tests were administered to experimental and control classes to provide measures of cognitive ability and self-esteem. Classroom discussion was analyzed using video recordings to assess critical thinking and dialogue. The perceptions of students, teachers and head-teachers were analyzed using open-ended questionnaires, adding a qualitative dimension to the research.

The first two methods used a traditional pre–post experimental design. Standardized data was collected from 177 children on a cognitive abilities test and 186 children on a self-esteem test. Discussion in six other classes was video recorded. Following baseline measurements, one group participated in one hour of Philosophical Inquiry each week using the Thinking Through Philosophy program, while the matched control group followed their usual curriculum. Both groups were then retested under the same conditions. The Cognitive Ability Tests (CAT)[27] measured reasoning ability for each student through the use of multiple-choice questions while the Myself-as-a-Learner Scale (MALS)[28] provided a measure of students' perceptions of their academic self-esteem. As the school district refused to accept random sampling for this study, the intervention schools were to some degree self-selected, but not on the basis of highest motivation or best organization. All control schools and classes subsequently became involved in the second phase of implementation.

Follow-up cognitive testing took place 16 months later to compare pre-intervention and post-intervention results. A highly significant average gain per experimental student of six standardized points was found using the Cognitive Abilities Test[29]. There were no gains in the cognitive ability scores of the control group. The results indicated that even one hour of inquiry each week could have an impact on children's reasoning ability. Importantly, gains in cognitive ability at the age of eleven years are highly correlated with performance in national tests when students are aged sixteen years[30]. See Figure 8.1 for a graphic display.

Students rated themselves on Myself-as-a-Learner Scale statements, such as 'I need lots of help with my work', on a five-point scale. Pre-initiative scores were obtained and the procedure repeated seven months later as a posttest measure. A significant difference between the pre- and posttest total MALS scores for the experimental pupils[31] suggested that the program had contributed to academic self-esteem, a finding supported by questionnaire perceptions from the students[32].

Video recordings of classroom discussion of a Greek fable were used to evaluate the effects of Thinking Through Philosophy on classroom discussion[33]. The teacher read out the story and explored its meaning through discussion with the class. A number of 'prompt questions' were provided to each teacher to get discussion started. After experimental

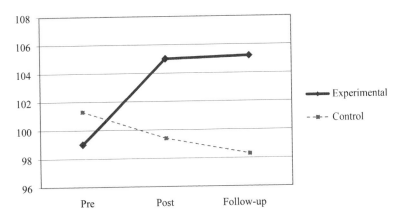

Figure 8.1 Cognitive abilities test scores for P4C and controls at pre, post and follow-up (with data from Topping and Trickey, 2007)

classes were involved in a weekly Thinking Through Philosophy lesson, the teachers repeated the same task seven months later. Both sets of videos were scored using a structured observation schedule. The rate of students' supporting their views with reasons doubled; teachers increased their use of open-ended follow-up questions; the percentage of time that students were speaking (compared to the percentage of time that the teacher was speaking) increased from 41% to 66% and the length of student utterances in the experimental classes increased on average by 58%. Control classes were also video recorded pre and post and there were no significant changes. The analysis of the video recordings of the classroom discussions provided evidence of increased participation, increased elaboration of responses by the children and an increase in the use of open-ended, follow-up teacher questions.

The perceptions of students were obtained through an analysis of questionnaires completed six months after the start of the intervention, which was continuing. Additional observations were also obtained from principal teachers six months after the start of the intervention and from participating teachers throughout the support meetings. Responses to the student questionnaires on nine open-ended questions were assigned to categories that reflected consistent themes in the responses. There was evidence of development in communication skills, confidence and concentration and the data suggested that the inquiry process helped students self-manage impulsivity.[32]

Evidence of socioemotional impact was strengthened by the consistency of student responses across different questions in the questionnaire and consistency between student, class teacher and head-teacher perceptions. There was also consistency in findings triangulated from different evaluation methodologies. For example, the questionnaires and the video analysis of classroom discussion both provided evidence of increased participation of pupils in classroom discussion and student perceptions of increased confidence matched gains measured on the standardized test of academic self-esteem.

Observations of social/emotional impact were consistent with subsequent studies[34], where teachers and students have reported a positive influence on students' confidence to speak, listening skills and self-esteem. In one controlled study[35], teachers reported a positive effect of P4C on the confidence of children in questioning and reasoning not only in P4C sessions but also in other lessons. Improvements in students' behavior included a reduction in bullying and other anti-social behaviors, which was attributable to increased communication and cooperation.

The cognitive element of the Thinking Through Philosophy study was subsequently replicated in the United States in a study in Huntsville (near Houston), Texas[36]. The Cognitive Abilities Test was again administered as a pretest and a posttest, but to randomly selected experimental groups (N = 363, 186 seventh graders + 177 eighth graders) and control groups (N = 177, 79 seventh graders + 98 eighth graders). The students in the experimental group engaged in philosophy lessons via structured collaborative inquiry in their language arts classes for one hour per week. The control group received the standard language arts curriculum in that hour. Seventh-grade students who had experienced the P4C program showed significant gains relative to the seventh-grade control group at a high level of statistical significance, but the eighth-grade experimental students did not show such gains over their control group. It transpired that the seventh-grade teachers started the program early in the school year and continued it for a period of 22 to 26 weeks, while the eighth-grade teachers started much later and used the program for only 4 to 10 weeks. The findings suggested that the P4C program must involve students in activities for a significant period of time before the program shows measurable results. See Figure 8.2 for a graphic display for the seventh graders.

In England, a randomized controlled trial involving 48 elementary schools found a positive impact of Philosophy for Children on reading and math attainment[34]. In this Education Endowment Foundation funded evaluation, teachers were trained by the Society for the Advancement of Philosophical Enquiry and Reflection in Education (SAPERE). Students averaged one period of P4C per week for 12 months from January until December.

Implementation was adequate or better in 14 P4C schools (64%), but in 8 P4C schools implementation was not adequate. While the

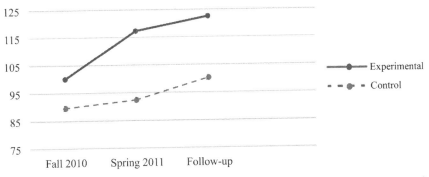

Figure 8.2 Cognitive abilities test scores for 7th grade P4C and controls at pre, post and follow-up (with data from Fair et al., 2015)

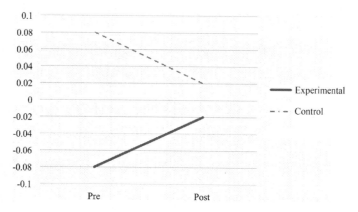

Figure 8.3 All pupils reading mean pre–post standardized Z-score (effect size = 0.12) (with data from Gorard, Siddiqui and See, 2017)

schools were diverse, the largest impact on reading and math was found with disadvantaged students (those eligible for Free School Meals – FSM). Analyses of the Cognitive Abilities Test results found a smaller positive impact compared with gains in reading and math. However, non-FSM pupils gained much more on CAT compared to FSM pupils. Teachers reported that the overall success of the intervention depended on incorporating P4C into the timetable, to avoid the risk that the program would be crowded out. Teachers and pupils generally reported that P4C had a positive influence on student's social and communication skills. See Figures 8.3–8.6 for a graphic display.

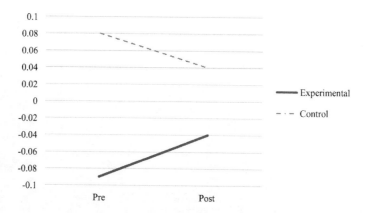

Figure 8.4 All pupils mathematics mean pre–post standardized Z-score (effect size = 0.10), (with data from Gorard, Siddiqui and See, 2017)

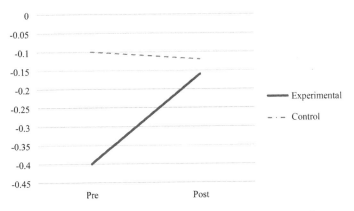

Figure 8.5 FSM pupils reading mean pre–post standardized Z-score (effect size = 0.29), (with data from Gorard, Siddiqui and See, 2017)

What Research Methods Are Best for Evaluating Effects of Philosophy for Children?

There were several differences between the Education Endowment Foundation study and the Thinking Through Philosophy study. These included the duration of the projects, materials used, training and support, consistency of timetabling and school district interest. Discrepancies in findings also support Burden and Nichols[26] assertion that it may be unrealistic to attempt to replicate pre–post evaluation designs in complex real-life situations such as classrooms that are inevitably simultaneously influenced by large numbers of volatile confounding variables.

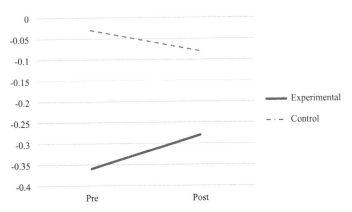

Figure 8.6 FSM pupils maths mean pre-post standardised Z-score (effect size = 0.20)

This sentiment overlaps with a reservation expressed previously by Slade[37], who concluded that standardized tests such as the New Jersey Test of Reasoning Skills may be too narrow and that evaluations should place more emphasis on the analysis of classroom dialogues. Reznitskaya[38] similarly argued that standardized tests were limited in evaluating gains in argumentation and reasoning during Philosophy for Children. It was for that reason that the Thinking Through Philosophy study broadened its methods to include video recording and student questionnaire analysis.

Conversely, Salmon[39] suggested that qualitative methods avoid questions of generalization and transferability and are less helpful to the reader in making judgments of whether studies have been successful or worthless. This latter argument seems to be more consistent with Sternberg's earlier observations. Experimental or quasi-experimental research offers the advantage of exploration of causal relationships between two variables. The debate over qualitative versus quantitative evaluation of P4C is part of a more general debate that has been discussed in detail elsewhere[40,41,42]. The application of a predominantly positivistic cognitive psychology approach to critically evaluate a philosophical process may reflect a tension between 'philosophical uncertainty' and the 'empirical truths of cognitive psychology'. Robson[41] suggested that researchers should be pragmatic and advocated mixed methods according to what best fit any particular study (as was the case in the evaluation of Thinking Through Philosophy).

Sustainability

There have been very few longitudinal studies that have followed up the effects of Philosophy for Children over time. This is generally true of educational research, but short-term positive effects may wash out and 'sleeper' gains may take years to show[10]. Investigators need to be mindful of Hawthorne effects arising with a novel and enthusiastically introduced program that may heighten initial positive outcomes, but gains may prove difficult to generalize to other contexts or sustain in the longer term. Thinking skill interventions usually lack sustainability data. The Thinking Through Philosophy study was an exception in that experimental and control students were tracked down in their high schools after completion of the initial study in elementary schools.

This follow-up study[43] found that the previous gains in cognitive ability had been sustained through two years of high school education despite the lack of any obvious additional experience of philosophical inquiry.

A longitudinal study of the long-term impact of P4C is being conducted in Madrid[44], tracking children over a period of 20 years. A group trained in the P4C program were matched with a control group. Data on cognitive, non-cognitive and academic achievements were collected at three time points, at ages 8, 11/12, and 16. Preliminary analyses indicate that the program had positive impacts on general cognitive ability (ES = 0.44) and that after ten years P4C promoted an average advantage of half a standard deviation in general cognitive ability (≈ 7 IQ points). Although the study was long-term and involved matched controls, students were not randomized and the results from this preliminary analysis should therefore be treated with caution.

Overall Conclusions About the Effects of Philosophy for Children

Sutcliffe has commented[45] that, despite the range of materials used and the diverse training of facilitators, evaluations of Philosophy for Children have proved steadily positive. A similar conclusion was arrived at in Australia by Millet and Tapper[46]. This chapter also notes the international breadth of evaluations that have taken place in America, Europe, Asia[47] and Australia, supporting positive findings. It should be remembered that Philosophy for Children was originally conceived to be applied across a period of several years, whereas evaluations tend to take place over a considerably shorter period. This raises the question of whether longer intervention periods would strengthen the effect of the process. In addition, Lipman's caveat should be kept in mind that the program is only as good as the induction of teachers into the practice[1]. Nevertheless, the consistency of findings over time suggests that P4C is likely to have a positive effect on reasoning and the quality of classroom discussion. It may not be possible to assert that use of the P4C process will always lead to positive outcomes since implementation integrity can be highly variable. However, a range of evidence has been reported in this review that indicates, given certain conditions, children can gain significantly both academically and socially through this type of interactive process.

References

1. M. Lipman, A. M. Sharp and F. Oscanyon. *Philosophy in the classroom*. 1980. Philadelphia, PA: Temple University Press.
2. R. E. Nisbett. *Mindware: Tools for smart thinking*. 2015. New York, NY: Farrer, Straus and Giroux.
3. S. Higgins, et al., *A meta-analysis of the impact of the implementation of thinking skills approaches on pupils*. October 2005. London: EPPI-Center, University of London.
4. S. Higgins, D. Kokotsaki and R. Coe, *The teaching and learning toolkit technical appendices*. July 2012. London: Education Endowment Foundation/Sutton Trust.
5. P. C. Abrami et al., Instructional interventions affecting critical thinking skills and disposition: A stage 1 meta-analysis. *Review of Educational Research*, December 2008, vol. 78, issue 4, pp. 1102–1134.
6. D. M. Romney and M. T. Samuels. A meta-analytic evaluation of Feuerstein's Instrumental Enrichment program. *Educational and Child Psychology*, 2001, vol. 18 issue 4, pp. 19–34.
7. R. Feuerstein et al., *Instrumental Enrichment: An intervention programme for cognitive modifiability*. 1980, Baltimore, MD: University Park Press.
8. P. Adey and M. Shayer. *Really raising standards*. 1994. London: Routledge.
9. L. Endler and T. Bond. Changing science outcomes: Cognitive acceleration in a US setting. *Research in Science Education*, 2008, vol. 38, issue 2, pp. 149–166.
10. C. McGuinness. *From thinking skills to thinking classrooms*. 1999. London: Department for Employment and Education.
11. P. Cleghorn. *Thinking through philosophy*. 2002. Blackburn, England: Educational Printing Services.
12. D. Schon. *The reflective practitioner*. 1983. New York, NY. Basic Books.
13. J. MacBeath. *Schools must speak for themselves: The case for school self-evaluation*. 1999. London: Routledge Falmer.
14. B. Joyce and B. Showers. *Student achievement through staff development*. 1988. New York: Longman.
15. R. Sternberg and K. Bhana. Synthesis of research on the effectiveness of intellectual skills programs: Snake oil remedies or miracle cures? *Educational Leadership*, 1996, vol. 44, issue 2, pp. 60–67.

16. R. W. Karras. Final evaluation of the pilot program in philosophical reasoning in Lexington elementary schools 1978–79. *Thinking*, 1979, vol. 1, issue 3–4, pp. 26–32.

17. V. C. Shipman. Evaluation replication of the Philosophy for Children program – Final report. *Thinking*, 1983, vol. 5, issue. 1, pp. 45–57.

18. J. Iorio, M. Weinstein and J. Martin. A review of District 24's Philosophy for Children program. *Thinking*, 1984, vol. 5, issue 2, pp. 28–35.

19. Institute for the Advancement of Philosophy for Children. *Research in Philosophy for Children*. Available at: www.montclair.edu/cehs/academics/centers-and-institutes/iapc/research/cognitive-skills/ [19 November 2018].

20. E. A. Morante and A. Ulesky, Assessment of reasoning abilities. *Educational Leadership*, September 1984, vol. 42, issue 1, pp. 71–74.

21. H. A. Butler, et al., The Halpern Critical Thinking Assessment and real-world outcomes: Cross-national applications. *Thinking Skills and Creativity*, Aug 2012, vol. 7, issue 2, pp. 112–121.

22. R. Sternberg. How can we teach intelligence? *Educational Leadership*, 1984, vol. 42, issue 1, pp. 38–48.

23. S. Trickey and K. J. Topping. Philosophy for Children: A systematic review. *Research Papers in Education*, 2004, vol. 19, issue 3, pp. 363–378.

24. F. Garcia-Moriyon, I. Robollo and R. Colom. Evaluating Philosophy for Children: A meta-analysis. *Thinking*, 2005, vol. 17, issue 4, pp. 14–22.

25. R. Slavin. Best evidence synthesis: An alternative to meta-analysis and traditional reviews. *Educational Reviewer*, 1986, vol. 15, issue 9, pp. 5–11.

26. R. Burden and L. Nichols. Evaluating the process of introducing a thinking skills programme into the secondary school curriculum. *Research Papers in Education*, 2000, vol. 15, issue 3, pp. 293–306.

27. D. F. Lohman, R. L. Thorndike and E. P. Hagen. *Cognitive Abilities Test*. 2001. Windsor, England: NFER-Nelson.

28. R. Burden. *Myself as a Learner Scale*. 2000. Windsor, England: NFER-Nelson.

29. K. J. Topping and S. Trickey. Collaborative philosophical enquiry for school children: Cognitive effects at 10–12 years. *British Journal of Educational Psychology*, 2007, issue 77, pp. 271–288.

30. I. J. Deary et al., Intelligence and educational achievement. *Intelligence*, 2007, vol. 35, issue 1, pp. 13–21.

31. S. Trickey and K. J. Topping. Collaborative philosophical enquiry for school children: Socio-emotional effects at 11–12 years. *School Psychology International*, 2006, vol. 27, issue 5, pp. 599–614.

32. S. Trickey and K. J. Topping. Collaborative philosophical enquiry for school children: Participant evaluation at 11 years. *Thinking*, 2007, vol. 18, issue 3, pp. 23–34.

33. K. J. Topping and S. Trickey. Impact of philosophical enquiry on school students' interactive behaviour. *International Journal of Thinking Skills and Creativity*, 2007, vol. 2, issue 2, pp. 73–84.

34. S. Gorard, N. Siddiqui and B. H. See. Can Philosophy for Children improve primary school attainment? *Journal of Philosophy of Education*, February 2017, vol. 51, issue 1, pp. 5–22.

35. N. Siddiqui, S. Gorard and B. H. See. *Non-cognitive impacts of Philosophy for Children. Project report.* 2017. Durham, England: School of Education, Durham University.

36. F. Fair et al., Socrates in the schools from Scotland to Texas: Replicating a study on the effects of a Philosophy for Children program. *Journal of Philosophy in Schools*, 2015, vol. 2, issue 1, pp. 18–37.

37. C. Slade. Creative and critical thinking. An evaluation of Philosophy for Children. *Analytic Teaching*, 1992, vol. 13, issue 1, pp. 25–36.

38. A. Reznitskaya. Empirical research in Philosophy for Children: Limitations and new directions. *Thinking*, 2005, vol. 17, issue 4, pp. 4–13.

39. P. Salmon. How do we recognise good research? *The Psychologist*, 2003, vol. 16, issue 1, pp. 24–27.

40. P. Reason and J. Rowan. *Human inquiry: A sourcebook of new paradigm research.* 1981. Chichester, England: John Wiley.

41. C. Robson. *Real world research.* 1983. Oxford, England: Blackwell.

42. N. Mercer. The analysis of classroom talk: Methods and methodologies. *British Journal of Educational Psychology*, 2010, issue 80, pp. 1–14.

43. K. J. Topping and S. Trickey. Collaborative philosophical enquiry for school children: Cognitive gains at two-year follow-up. *British Journal of Educational Psychology*, 2007, vol. 77, pp. 781–796.

44. R. Colom, F. García Moriyón, C. Magro and E. Morilla. The long-term impact of Philosophy for Children: A longitudinal study (preliminary results). *Analytic Teaching and Philosophical Praxis*, 2014, vol. 35, issue 1, pp. 50–56.

45. R. Sutcliffe. The evaluation of Philosophy for Children in the UK. In B. Anderson (Ed.) *Philosophy for Children: Theories and praxis in teacher education*. 2017, p. 7. Abingdon, England: Routledge.

46. S. Millett and A. Tapper. The benefits of collaborative philosophical inquiry in schools. *Educational Philosophy and Theory*, 2012, vol. 44, issue 5, pp. 546–567.

47. T. K. Lim. New instruments to evaluate a P4C program. In E. Marsal, T. Dobashi and B. Weber (Eds.), *Children philosophize worldwide: Theoretical and practical concepts*. 2009. New York, NY: Peter Lang.

9

Evaluating Philosophical Inquiry

Teachers will tend to think about the formative purposes of evaluation – what can I find out which will help me see what parts of P4C worked and what parts did not? Then, it is not a case of rejecting the parts that did not work – instead, the teacher asks, 'How can these parts be improved and made to work – how should I change them for next time? Or was it the case that these parts only failed to work with a certain group of students, and would work with another group? Or only failed to work with this year's class but might work with next year's class?' As Dylan Wiliam said in 2017: 'Feedback functions formatively only if the information fed back to the learner is used by the learner in improving performance'[1].

By contrast, from a summative assessment perspective, the question is only about what works in the here and now. If an intervention has one bad evaluation report, it may never be used again. Where the intervention is a complex one like P4C, composed of many parts, this leaves a question about which parts were the least effective. It also leaves a question about how the P4C was implemented – was this done with high quality or were there uncontrolled factors that entered into the practice? Was implementation integrity or fidelity actually reported on?

Teachers are more likely to be interested in formative assessment. A previous chapter reported on the evaluation evidence in largely summative terms. In this chapter we will first focus on ways of evaluating formatively, through participant perceptions and then through observation, in ways relevant to the teacher's own classroom. This first part is for teachers who seek feedback on how their inquiries are progressing, having put an early toe into the P4C waters.

After that we will begin to consider ways of evaluating in more detail, considering the research design and then different ways of gathering data. This part is more aimed at teachers who are seeking to undertake a more serious research evaluation. It is more likely to be used by teachers engaged in a course that requires them to do a research project, or perhaps teachers who need to present their findings to the school district or a state or national conference.

Formative assessment yields data on different parts of the process, while summative data sometimes only yields data on the overall package – which of course leaves you not knowing what to change, and thus in danger of throwing the baby out with the bathwater. Perhaps the best approach would be to combine formative and summative assessment, and accumulate the strengths of both methods. But of course, this requires time, something of which teachers have very little.

There are certainly dangers in only gathering data by one means, measure or instrument. If you only collected student views, and they generally said they didn't like P4C, how would you know whether or not P4C had caused cognitive change in them? You could not assume one way or the other. We use this example because some researchers have done exactly that – and often tend to draw conclusions that are too broad. The concept of triangulation is important here. Despite its name, triangulation means using *two* (or more) different data gathering methods to see what similarity or difference there is between them. The term originated from navigation in sailing, where a location is determined by using the angles from two known points. So, whether you are evaluating formatively or summatively, try to obtain two or more forms of data.

So, let us turn now to gathering feedback from those who participated in the P4C project, primarily the students themselves.

Participant Perceptions

You can ask the students leading questions about their experiences, but remember you are likely to obtain more honest answers if you ask them anonymously. The leads some teachers into using a questionnaire.

The problem with a questionnaire is that you have little guarantee that the students are answering honestly. They might just be giving you the answers they think you want to hear. Additionally, if you give them response options on a scale, be sure that you do not include a center point, or this will become a favorite answer for students who can't be bothered to think about the question. Make the scale pretty wide and make sure its points are numbers between either end. The ends should have adjectival labels.

Against this, you can certainly ask the students about different parts of the P4C process (which were best, which were least good), about different outcomes (thinking better, getting on better with each other) and to what extent they used their thinking skills outside of the classroom (and indeed, outside of the school). You can also ask them how they would improve the process next time or for other students (shorter sessions, a longer set of sessions, more time devoted to one or other activity), and whether they would recommend the process to other students (compared to other lessons).

Alternatively, you could engage a smaller number of selected students in an individual interview. This is of course assuming that you have an infinite amount of time. You need to select the students to be interviewed randomly or representatively according to their distribution in terms of age, gender, ability, or other relevant criteria. Questions similar to those in the questionnaire would be good to use in the interview, but not so many. You are likely to get more accurate and detailed information this way (although the student is even more likely to tell you what he/she thinks you want to hear), and be more sharply aware of when students are making up answers of doubtful veracity.

In theory, by either of these means you will obtain the individual opinions of the students. Of course, P4C is a social process, so that might not be what you want. Another way of obtaining data is by group interview or, as it is sometimes called, focus groups. You might want all the students to be involved in several groups of 8–10 students, or you might want just some of the students to be involved. Either way, be sure you have selected the students for each focus group so that they are representative of the whole group, even if it means including some whose opinions you know will be negative. Of course, focus groups do have a social process also, so students in them might have their views changed by peer pressure (or because they realize their peers are correct). Consequently, you might find that there is a greater tendency towards eventual agreement from a focus group than there is with individual question-naires or interviews. That is one reason why you should try to have more than one, with different students.

Observation

Observation is arguably a more accurate method of determining what went on in P4C sessions, since you can do it early, in the middle and late in each session and in the cycle of sessions, thereby giving you a feeling for developments over time. Indeed, you can do it before the P4C project starts and again after it finishes. However, again you have a problem if you are the P4C session teacher and also the data gatherer. It is almost impossible to do both well at the same time. You might want to video the sessions and look at then after the session. You will get more accuracy this way, but this is dependent on the quality of the video and its associated soundtrack. It also takes more time, of course. Alternatively, you might ask a colleague to observe your session (perhaps on the basis that then you will observe one of their sessions).

Even more alternatively, you might want to engage the students themselves in observation of P4C. Obviously this will depend on the age and maturity of the students and how experienced they are in the P4C process. Additionally, you might want only a few selected students to be so engaged. But what a good opportunity to really learn more about P4C in practice – and what an effect it might have on the observer's own practice! The great advantage of involving students is that it reduces the workload on the already overstretched teacher.

Here we give some tools that are relevant to this task. They are adapted from the work of Cleghorn and Cleghorn[2]. All of them are also available in the book's Resource Website so you can print them off for immediate use.

Classroom Observation Sheet

This may be used either by a teacher reflecting on a philosophy ses-sion that has recently taken place, or more usefully, by a teacher who is using the program observing someone else facilitating a session. If the latter strategy is employed, subsequent discussion of the comments is an important part of the process. It is the simplest method because the detail of anecdotal evidence can be written and shared with the teacher later, but there is a power in its simplicity. It is available in the book's Resource Website as Download 15 (adapted from Cleghorn and Cleghorn, 2005).

In observing the philosophy session, jot down strengths, weaknesses and points for discussion. Remember to note good comments by children, evidence or reasons given by children, linking of several ideas by an individual or several people, the range of questions by children and whether the group has moved forward through dialogue. What threads were followed by the facilitator?

These are the headings given in the classroom observation sheet:

The Calming Exercise:
The Stimulus:
Individual/Pair/Group Work:
The Enquiry Through Dialogue: (This should be the longest section and most detailed)
General Comments:

Assessing Classroom Dialogue

Use of this sheet can help show the progress made in effecting good dialogue. The sheet must be completed by a person other than the facilitator but who also is familiar with the program. It is a simple tool for use at the early stages of introducing inquiry and building a community. Making pupils familiar with the criteria in the beginning stages is helpful in letting them develop the concept of what constitutes good dialogue. Video record ten minutes of the dialogue part of a session then analyze it later. The Classroom Dialogue sheet is available in the book's Resource Website (see Download 16).

Class: Duration:		Date:	
Behavior		**Tally marks**	**Total**
Student			
1. Occurrence of pupils asking a question.			
2. Occurrence of student supporting their view/ opinion with a reason.			
3. Occurrence of a student agreeing or disagreeing with the view of another pupil, and giving a reason.			

(Continued)

4. Occurrence of student offering a reviewing or evaluating comment.
5. Occurrence of student directly addressing another pupil.

Teacher

6. Occurrence of teacher asking a question requiring a one word or factual response.
7. Occurrence of teacher asking an open-ended question. (This includes follow-up questions).

Adapted from Cleghorn and Cleghorn, 2005

Assessing Philosophical Inquiry

This tool covers both the rational structure for exploring ideas through dialogue (the 'technical' aspects of what constitutes good dialogue) and also the moral structure, which includes those aspects of emotional intelligence which by their nature allow good dialogue to take place. For example, the former includes such things as supporting one's assertions with evidence and asking open-ended questions, while the latter includes respecting the ideas of others and using positive body language to encourage others.

The sheet can be used in several ways. It can be used in similar fashion to the last two, by teachers' reflecting on the work of their own group or by a teacher observing a colleague. This sheet can also be used with pupils, allowing them to reflect on, and evaluate, their own work. It is important to spend time with pupils looking at each point and discussing what it means in practice. This focus on the criteria is very useful in helping children to understand what is considered 'good dialogue' and why. Using it as a formative assessment tool is a robust method of dialogical development. It was developed, with permission, from work by Roger Sutcliffe. It is also available in the book's Resource Website as Download 17 (adapted from Cleghorn and Cleghorn, 2005).

A score can be put against each point:

Social Skills (Ethos)
0 = Hardly ever, 1 = Some, sometimes, 2 = Most, most of the time, 3 = Almost all the time

1. Did students respond to the questions being asked?
2. Did students focus their attention on the speaker?

3. Did students avoid interrupting the speaker?
4. Did the group encourage each other to speak?
5. Did students respond to the previous speaker?
6. Were the contributions brief and to the point?
7. Did students recall the ideas of others and name them?
8. Did people try to build on the idea of others?
9. Did students listen to ideas different from their own?
10. Was there a willingness for people to change their minds?

Thinking Together
0 = Not observed, 1 = Observed once, 2 = Observed a few times, 3 = Observed often

1. Did students ask open and inviting questions?
2. Did anyone ask for clarification?
3. Did students question assumptions?
4. Did anyone ask for examples or evidence?
5. Did students ask for reasons or criteria?
6. Did anyone give an example or counter-example?
7. Did anyone give a reason or justification?
8. Did people offer or explore alternative viewpoints?
9. Did students make comparisons or analogies?
10. Did students make distinctions?

Critical Thinking Matrix

This tool provides a detailed look at critical thinking and what actions and behaviors constitute good critical thinking. It can be used in several ways. It is available in the book's Resource Website (see Download 18).

The first use is to gain a broad impression of the quality of critical thinking in a group or class. To do this, read and become familiar with the criteria in general terms. In listening to the group (class), notice when various criteria are exhibited. By seeing whether the bulk of comments heard are related to columns one, two or three, an impression of the general quality of the critical thinking can be gained.

The second, more sophisticated use provides a more accurate picture of the quality of the thinking, and also can be related to formative assessment. First, copy the blank matrix. Then put a tally mark in the appropriate box when an example of one of the criteria in that box is heard. At the end of the lesson, get a score by giving 5 points for every mark in column three, 3 points for marks in column two, and 1 for marks in column one. Use the information formatively by discussing with the group where the bulk of the marks fell, and what this means in terms of specific criterion.

Explain and discuss the matrix fully, so pupils are aware of what constitutes good critical thinking. Use examples from their own comments, and let *them* recall examples. In this way, the students will seek to improve in the next dialogue, and deliberately employ better thinking.

	Not skilled	Competent	Expert
Clarity	No clarifying questions. Arguments not clear. Muddled ideas. Does not define ideas or arguments.	Asks for some clarification. Tries to be clear in expressing ideas. Sometimes follows a line of argument.	Asks clarifying questions. Clear ideas expressed. Follows a line of argument. Defines things clearly. Clarifies meaning aloud.
Coherence	No linking ideas. Has diverse ideas. Decisions made on 'whims', not based on information. Cannot summarize group dialogue.	Can take 2 or 3 ideas or pieces of information and integrate them. Beginning to be able to summarize.	Puts several ideas together. Unifies. Integrates pieces of information to make a decision. Can summarize well. Exhibits a structure to an argument.
Accuracy	Not aware of contexts. Cannot identify irrelevance. Evidence and arguments are unclear and imprecise.	Makes effort to define. Is aware of irrelevance and usually ignores it. Makes effort to be precise.	Defines terms appropriate to the context. Can identify and ignore irrelevance. Tries to give precise information and descriptions.

(Continued)

	Not skilled	**Competent**	**Expert**
Fairness	Is biased. Works only from habitual ideas. Not interested in other's views. Ignores or is not aware of others' feelings. Is not aware of a broad range of issues.	Is aware of concept of open-mindedness. Tries to be open minded and examine issues. Makes efforts to consider others' views and take account of their feelings.	Is open minded. Examines all issues. Is open to alternative views. Considers other people's views. Exhibits emotional intelligence (takes account of others' feelings and understanding).
Originality	Doesn't show originality. Reticent to try new ideas /methods. Doesn't seek alternative solutions.	Sometimes intentionally seeks alternatives. Sometimes shows original ideas. Beginning to open up to new ideas/ solutions.	Seeks alternative solutions/ conclusions. Offers original ideas and arguments. Has a willingness to try new methods.
Strategies	No organizational strategies shown. Doesn't show problem-solving strategies. Cannot begin to organize.	Exhibits some organizational strategies. Beginning to draw sequences from data. Problem-solving ideas are discussed and tested.	Uses various strategies to organize information. Follows problem-solving steps. Exhibits logical patterns of analyzing information. Can work in the abstract.
Critical Questioning / Attitude	Accepts 'first answers and explanations'. Accepts assumptions. Has a narrow perspective. Does not probe for depth.	Is aware of the importance of reasons and evidence. Beginning to question options and assumptions. Showing more awareness of alternative views.	Seeks evidence. Probes explanations. Questions assumptions. Looks for alternative views. Shows an eagerness to enquire further.

Adapted from Cleghorn and Cleghorn, 2005.

Fisher[3] suggests using video to support observational techniques. He notes that there are several ways of observing, with either the teacher conducting the analysis, the participants self-analyzing their own contributions or those of others, or a combination of the two. He also notes that video can be very useful for formative feedback, in that brief sections of video showing a student doing something very well can be highly instructive for all the class.

Where a video is available for analysis, there are several options:

1. Tracking the whole discussion with all children (a daunting task)
2. Tracking one cognitive or discourse feature (a much easier thing to do)
3. Tracking one student (or a small group) through the discussion
4. Tracking the *spoken* contributions of all participants (perhaps noting gender)
5. Analyzing the ratio and length of conversations between students and teachers
6. Focusing on particular episodes – perhaps a very good episode and a poor episode.

Research Design

Participant perceptions tend to be gathered only at the end of a project. However, observations may be gathered before a project starts, after it finishes or at any point in between. Because evaluation is basically about measuring the degree of change, observations are a stronger form of research design when data is gathered pre and post (before and after) the project. Perceptions tend to be gathered post only.

However, if your measure is not norm-referenced (standardized), you will have no way of telling whether the children would have made those pre–post changes anyway, irrespective of the project. (Standardization refers to averages for hundreds of children from all over the country.) Even if your measure is norm-referenced (like a standardized reading test), unless your results are spectacularly better than 'normal' rates of gain, you still won't have proof that the children could only have made those gains with the help of the project.

So, you really need to compare the progress of your project students with the progress of a similar local group who has not been involved in the project. This other group would be known as a 'control' group. Two problems arise. First, especially in an elementary school, the control class will be taught by another teacher. We know that teacher effects can be very large in either direction. So, you may only be measuring the effect of the teacher. Secondly, is it fair to compare a group doing extra thinking work with a group not doing any extra thinking work? Obviously the first group are likely to do better. So, can the control group be a least devoting a similar amount of time to a somewhat similar activity?

Nonetheless, the preferred research design is a pre–post control group design. This is described as an experimental design, since it has most chance of providing convincing evidence that the project has an effect.

When you operate a project, you may find that some students opt out. Can you use these opted out students as a control group? Well, no, not really – since they have self-selected to opt out, they are a biased group who are not really comparable to the experimental group. But this might be the best you can do, in which case, do not call them a control group, but a 'comparison group'.

To get a true control group, you would list all the students eligible for the project, then select them randomly for participation by tossing a coin or some such. The only problem with this is that you might end up dividing classes, which would not be operationally feasible. So often you will choose experimental and control groups by the whole class. Remember that the control group can be considered a 'wait' group, who will experience the P4C project at a later date. One of the problems with true control groups is that their use involves denying a service or facility to people who clearly seem to be in need of it. It can be argued that until you have demonstrated that the project has worked satisfactorily by using the control group, you don't actually know whether you are denying the control group anything worthwhile, but this logical contention does not tend to go down that well with caring teachers. The wait group idea helps get around this problem.

Whatever you choose to do, some attempt to guard against the Hawthorne Effect is necessary – the effect whereby the clients of an intervention show brief improvement purely because some attention is being paid to them and there is some element of novelty about the proceedings, quite irrespective of the actual nature of the intervention.

Another possible source of embarrassment is the John Henry Effect – where the control group, alerted to the fact that somebody considers them to be in need but is not providing anything for them, determines to improve anyway, and does so without apparent outside intervention.

Measures

The first thing to remember is that you don't have to do all the work. It would be paradoxical to operate a project involving lots of peer interaction and then resort to purely teacher-driven methods of evaluation. It is perfectly possible to have the participating students themselves collect data. Think about whether students can interview each other. Can you have the students apply tests to each other as well? Remember you can have the students score them. Maybe you can even have some students doing the data analysis as a special project. The project coordinator's time is limited, so decisions have to be made about how many and which evaluative measures are going to be applied to helper and helped respectively.

There are various basic requirements of any measures you seek to use. Economy of cost in materials and of time in administration and scoring are two obvious considerations. The measure needs to be reliable, in the sense of not being susceptible to wild, random fluctuations or erratic guesswork. It also needs to be valid, that is, one must be assured that it actually measures what it is purporting to measure. Of equal importance, it needs to be relevant to the processes in question. Last, but by no means least, the measure must generate information that is analyzable. A vast quantity of impressionistic opinion may be fascinating to the project organizers, but will not enable them to communicate their findings to others in a clear and credible way.

Tests

P4C is nothing if not personal. Problems tend to be solved jointly as much as individually, and help is more or less always at hand. The relationship and the speed of progress through the process is highly idiosyncratic. To attempt to assess the impact of an experience of this kind by the use of some sort of test wherein the students sit in isolation in serried ranks and wrestle without help with some alien task, seems logically to be something of a nonsense – or is it?

If you wish to determine whether P4C produced results that will spread and endure outside of the situation, then the application of a test could be construed as a usefully stringent measure of generalization. However, remember that whatever the reliability of the test quoted in the manual may be, with a small and idiosyncratically selected group of children with learning difficulties, reliability may be actually considerably less. While the use of tests may show substantial rates of gain taking the project group as a whole, individual results may seem so implausible that they should not be given much weight.

Norm-referenced tests allow a student's performance to be compared with that of many others in various parts of the country. Criterion-referenced tests allow a student's performance to be compared with his or her own previous performance or some other benchmark of performance relevant to the curriculum. The first compares the student with other students, and the second compares the student's performance with a pre-determined criterion of skill acquisition. All tests have inherent problems. They may provoke anxiety in some students, making their individual results largely meaningless. For others, the unreality and apparent purposelessness of the exercise produces equally strange results. Students may copy from each other if this is not prevented. What the test means to the student might be quite different to what it means for the teacher.

Examples of norm-referenced tests that have been used to evaluate P4C include the New Jersey Test of Reasoning Skills, Cornell Critical Thinking Test, Whimbey Analytical Skills Inventory and the Cognitive Abilities Test[4], the Halpern Critical Thinking Assessment (HCTA)[5] and the Cognitive Ability Tests (CAT)[6]. On the socioemotional side, the MALS (Myself-as-a-Learner Scale) has been used[7]. Of course, you might want to investigate any improvement in standard curriculum subjects as well as cognitive gains, so you also might want to use a reading test, or a mathematics test or both.

By contrast, the advantage of criterion-referenced tests is that they can much more flexibly reflect the reality of P4C (and you can make them up yourself). Their disadvantage is that comparison with national norms is no longer possible, and the absence of that vast, distant quasi-'control' group means that much more emphasis must be placed on achieving an adequate evaluation design. Basically, a criterion-referenced test checks whether the helped students have learned what they have been taught. While this may sound simple and logical, such tests might not give information on how well the students can generalize new skills to other areas, unless this is built into the structure of the test. Nor may it be easy to obtain any idea of whether the student is accelerating at a rate that will eventually enable them to catch up with the average student.

Computer programs have become available to assist the teacher with the management of information about learning in the classroom. Forms of computerized curriculum-based measurement and norm-referenced measurement can be both delivered to the student and scored by the computer, which then analyzes the results and advises the teacher of the outcome (and sometimes the diagnostic implications for action). Where such tests have a very large item bank, every test presented to every student on every occasion is different, which not only minimizes student cheating but also enables the tests to be taken very frequently without scores being inflated by practice effects as students get to learn the test content. Norm-referenced tests are of course not as closely tied to P4C as curriculum-based tests, but can still form a useful measure of student progress in terms of generalization of skills to novel content.

Other Measures

A crude naturalistic indicator of improved behavior might be a reduced incidence of disciplinary referrals. There may be evidence of reductions in bullying, fighting and vandalism. Where data on these are not already collected through existing record systems, it may be worthwhile to have adults in regular contact with target children complete some form of rating, either a specific checklist of problem behaviors or more generalized observational assessments of problem behavior.

There are a range of other measures, which may have the virtue of seeming quicker and easier, but that also raise more serious questions about their relationship to everyday reality. Some form of sociometry is a particular favorite, on a before and after basis, to discern whether pairs develop any greater preference for each other on paper and pencil completion of peer preference lists. Attempts can be made to tap the more generalized attitudes of pairs to each other, and this could be done verbally on an individual or group basis, or with no fewer threats to reliability via some form of simple questionnaire of controlled readability.

Generalization and Maintenance

With all these measures, the issue of generalization needs to be addressed. Is it enough to have some form of evidence that gains have occurred that are specific to the pair and the situation or context, or is it reasonable to expect these gains to generalize to ordinary classroom sessions, free-play times, or perhaps even to the community and home environments beyond the school boundary? Do we expect these gains to generalize to other situations, to other (untargeted) skills or problems, to other resource materials or to other helping or helped students? If we do expect this, how are we to measure it? Most difficult of all, how are we to measure it easily?

The other thorny question is that of long-term duration of gains made. Many teaching programs have shown reasonable results in the short-term, but the gains produced have often 'washed out' in comparison to control groups at two-year follow-up. So, some form of follow-up evaluation is important, preferably together with follow-up of a control or comparison group. Such an exercise is often made difficult by the loss of subjects from one or both groups, called sample attrition. Remember to try to follow-up your project students to see if their gains have maintained over time (and perhaps over changes in school or beyond). This is difficult and very time-consuming to do, but is vital if we are to see any long-term effect. On the other hand, it is also reasonable to ask how long you can sensibly expect a relatively brief and lightweight intervention to continue to demonstrate an impact on the highly complex and cumulative learning process.

Analysis of Data

There is a great difference between statistical and educational significance. Where a very large sample is used, statistical significance is much easier to achieve. Where a very large number of different outcome measures are used, the chances are that one or two will show statistically significant changes irrespective of any real impact of the project. If a project with large samples produces gains that are only just statistically significant, searching questions need to be asked about the educational significance of the results. Was it worth all that time and effort for such a small skill increment?

Particularly if your sample size is small, it may be better to rely on effect sizes as a measure of impact. Take the mean posttest score, subtract the mean pretest score, and divide by the standard deviation of the pretest scores. The result will hopefully be positive! If it is 0.2 or so, there is a small effect. If 0.5 or so, a moderate effect. If 0.8 or above, a large effect.

For those unsure of their competence in statistical analysis, or doubting the validity of the procedures, simple comparison of raw data on scattergrams or graphing of shifts in averages for groups gives a ready visual indication of changes. Certainly, the data is worth summarizing in this sort of way for feedback to the participants, who may be assumed to be statistically unsophisticated.

Evaluation Results Feedback and Dissemination

One of the disadvantages of complex data analysis is that it takes time, and very often early feedback of evaluation results to the project participants is highly desirable to renew their commitment and recharge their energies. A simple graph and/or brief table of average scores for the group are probably the best vehicle for this – remember, the results must be understood by the learners as well.

The unreliability of standardized tests makes giving individual test scores to the participants a risky business, and care must be taken throughout not to give undue emphasis to test data as distinct from other types. Any individual scores are probably best given in an individual meeting rather than in a group meeting situation, if at all.

Evaluation results have a number of other uses. Publicity via the local press, professional journals, curriculum bulletins or in-service meetings not only helps to disseminate good practice and help more children, it also serves to boost the morale of the project initiators and participants. The results may be useful to convince skeptics on the school staff, generate a wider interest and produce a more coherent future policy on peer assessment in the school.

The school governors will be interested, as should be various officers of the state or school district education authority. A demonstration of cost-effectiveness may elicit more tangible support. Associated services such as library services, advisory services, resource materials centers and so on might be drawn into the network of community support by a convincing evaluation report.

And so, to the final word. If you get results you don't like, you'll spend hours puzzling over them trying to explain them away. Make sure that if you get results you do like, you spend as much time and energy searching for other factors outside the project that could have produced them. If you don't spot them, someone else might – and probably will!

References

1. D. Wiliam. *Embedded formative assessment (strategies for classroom assessment that drive student engagement and learning).* Second edition. 2017. Bloomington, IN: Solution Tree Press.
2. P. Cleghorn and D. Cleghorn. *Thinking about personal and social development.* 2005. Blackburn, England: Eprint. ISBN 1 904904 51 3.
3. R. Fisher. *Teaching thinking: Philosophical enquiry in the classroom.* Fourth edition. 2013. London: Bloomsbury Academic.
4. E. A. Morante and A. Ulesky. Assessment of reasoning abilities. *Educational Leadership*, September 1984, vol. 42, issue 1, pp. 71–74.
5. H. A. Butler, et al. The Halpern Critical Thinking Assessment and real-world outcomes: Cross-national applications. *Thinking Skills and Creativity*, Aug 2012, vol. 7, issue 2, pp. 112–121.
6. F. Lohman, R. L. Thorndike and E. P. Hagen. *Cognitive Abilities Test.* 2001. Windsor, England: NFER-Nelson.
7. R. Burden. *Myself as a Learner Scale.* 2000. Windsor, England: NFER-Nelson.

10

Truth, Democracy and Classroom Communities of Inquiry

In 1916 John Dewey wrote: 'Democracy has to be reborn anew every generation, and education is its midwife'[1] (p. 74). What indeed is the purpose of education? The educator's role in preparing students for life could be seen narrowly as training students in subject knowledge or could be extended more widely to include preparation to participate in society as a thinking citizen. This chapter considers communities of inquiry acting as classroom microcosms of larger democratic institutions and how these communities seek truth in an age sometimes referred to as the post-truth era[2]. Communities of inquiry prepare students for citizenship by promoting their communication, participation and reasoned discourse. In so doing, Philosophy for Children can improve the health of democracies.

At the start of Chapter 2 the suggestion was made that philosophical inquiry can be viewed as a structured search for truth using reason and good argument. We will explore what we mean by 'truth' in the context of education, democracy and citizenship. Several examples of how truth has been distorted will be given. Such distortions indicate a pressing need for students to critically consider information they are exposed to. We will also consider how the abstract concept of truth is complicated by psychological factors, such as unconscious bias.

Is Truth Problematic? Should Teachers Be Concerned?

In 2016, Oxford Dictionaries chose 'post-truth' as its word of the year[3]. Oxford Dictionaries defined post-truth as 'relating to or denoting circumstances in which objective facts are less influential in shaping public opinion than appeals to emotion and personal belief.' Truth, conversely, is that which is true or in accordance with fact or reality. The following January, the phrase 'alternative facts' was used by the United States President's campaign strategist. During a television interview, the strategist used the phrase in the context of defending a demonstrably false statement about attendance numbers at the president's inauguration[4]. Having been challenged over the term 'alternative facts' on one television channel, an interviewer on a more sympathetic television channel quickly suggested that alternative facts simply provide 'a different perspective'[5].

Truth can thus seem muddied. Public interest following the first alternative facts interview was reflected soon after when sales of George Orwell's book *1984*[6] spiked. This futuristic account of the manipulation of truth by an authoritarian regime was first published in 1949. Sales increased by 9,500%[7] as *1984* became one of the best sellers on Amazon. Orwell's totalitarian state used Newspeak as a language to diminish the range of thought by eliminating certain words. For example, Newspeak had no word for science[8].

Another contemporary example of 'muddying' truth came from the President's legal adviser, when he responded 'And when you tell me that, you know, he should testify because he's going to tell the truth and he shouldn't worry, well that's so silly because it's somebody's version of the truth. Not the truth.'[9]. He then added twice that 'truth isn't truth!' Such statements can hardly give students confidence about what is true and what is false.

In addition to post-truth and alternative facts, we also have 'fake news' that the Collins English Dictionary defines as 'false, often sensational information disseminated under the *guise* of news *reporting*'[10]. Fake news involves the deliberate publication of fictitious information on social media designed to mislead people for financial or political gain. In post-truth politics, facts become less important than emotions and personal beliefs. A previous president considered fake news to be a threat to democracy. During a press conference in 2016, that president suggested that 'If we are not serious about facts and what's true and what's not, if we can't discriminate between serious arguments and propaganda, then we have problems'[11]. The same president followed up his concerns about truth in his farewell speech[12] when he suggested 'Increasingly, we become so secure in our bubbles that we start accepting only information, whether it is true or not, that fits our opinions, instead of basing our opinions on the evidence that is out there.'

Is There a Threat to Healthy Democracies?

Fake news, and the proliferation of raw opinion that passes for news, creates confusion about the truth and increases polarization. Although there are concerns over people who readily form beliefs on the latest thing they have read, the larger problem is that fake news has the effect of getting people not to believe real things. They ignore the facts because nobody knows what is really true anyway[13].

Misinformation has always been around to confuse what is true. However, heavily automated electronic accounts, known as 'propaganda bots', now target propaganda (such as fake news stories) at those most vulnerable to misinformation. With the rise of social media, every click builds information that can predict our preferences and inclinations. Propaganda bots combine super-fast calculation capacities with specific personal information so that computational propaganda can deliver misinformation exactly to the people most vulnerable[14].

While most people see through false stories such as the existence of a Democrat pedophile ring being run from a Washington pizzeria, when these stories are supported by people in authority, such as the National Security Advisor, others, like the North Carolina gunmen who discharged his weapon in the pizzeria, will accept them uncritically. It has been estimated that about 8% of the adult population are willing to believe anything that sounds plausible and that fits their preconceptions[15]. People's hunger for information that suits their prejudices is powerful.

An illustration of events satisfying people's hunger for information consistent with their bias followed on from the president's comment on voter fraud when he declared, 'I'm afraid the election is going to be rigged. I have to be honest.'[16] and asserted that millions of ballots cast illegally by undocumented immigrants cost him the popular vote. This created a climate in which it was relatively easy for money to be made with a fake news story about fraudulent votes found in Ohio warehouse. That story took 15 minutes to write, was shared with six million people and earned about $5000 for the writer[17]. The reliance of Facebook and Google on advertising has meant they benefit from large numbers of 'hits' in response to sensational fake news stories.

A healthy democracy is threatened when untrue assertions are used to rally support for an agenda while denigrating as dishonest valid reporting pointing out falsehoods. For example, a travel ban on some nationalities was justified when the so-called 'Bowling Green massacre' was given as an example of domestic terrorism. The massacre had never happened, but the tweet got 2.4 million impressions[18] and was cited three times as justification for the ban[19].

It seems more important than ever that students have the critical thinking ability to question such stories. False news travels faster, further and deeper through the social network than true stories. False claims are 70% more likely to be shared on Twitter than the truth. True stories take about six times longer than false to reach 1500 people[20]. It takes a few minutes to create a viral story but hours of investigative work to debunk it. Never before has critical thinking been so necessary.

Conspiracy Theorists and What Is Truth

Truth was described at the start of this chapter as that which is true or in accordance with fact or reality. Conspiracy theories often produce hypotheses that contradict basic facts. Mass shootings have a particular tendency to attract conspiracy theorists. The radio host Alex Jones has claimed that the United States government perpetrated the 9/11 attacks and the tragedies at Columbine, Oklahoma City, Sandy Hook and the Boston Marathon[21]. He called the Sandy Hook school massacre a hoax. Conspiracy theorists were quick to accuse student survivors of the mass shooting in Parkland, Florida, as being actors in a conspiracy. The suggestion was that this event was actually staged for political reasons such as the establishment trying to take away people's guns. More than 111,000 Facebook users shared a post claiming the Parkland students were performers who exploit tragedies[22].

During the run-up to the last presidential election, a fake news story about the killing of an FBI agent who leaked Democrat emails received 1.6 million views over 10 days. The writer acknowledged that stories like this work because they fit into existing conspiracy theories. The writer also acknowledged that the story was total fiction. However, once posted, the story was readily picked up by sympathetic forums and 'spread like wildfire'[23]. The writer made money from the ads on his websites. There have been instances of false news from both sides of the political spectrum but sensationalist conspiratorial news appears overwhelmingly consumed by rightwing social network users in the United States[24].

Historical Concerns over Truth

Concerns about the veracity of information and 'what is true' are not a recent phenomenon. They have been rife throughout modern history, particularly when the stakes are high such as in war. As the U.S. Senator Hiram Warren Johnson is purported to have said in 1918: 'The first casualty when war comes is truth'[25]. For example, truth during the Viet Nam war became confused when what generals and politicians were saying differed markedly from what is being observed on the ground[26]. Similar examples could probably be taken from any modern conflict. What is very different now is the power of social media to amplify stories designed to sway opinion and mobilize emotion.

Concerns about Truth in Other Countries

A vigorous debate has taken place in the United Kingdom about Britain leaving the European Community. The claim that Britain sent £350 million a week to the European Union that could be spent on its National Health Service was emblazoned on a Brexit 'Vote Leave' supporting bus during the referendum campaign. The UK Statistics Authority found this claim misleading and undermining trust in statistics. Nevertheless, nearly half of the British public believed this Vote Leave claim[27]. Truth can be confusing!

It has been suggested that mistrust in facts was sown by climate change denial and insistence on creationism by some politicians and church leaders[8]. Calling climate change a hoax, despite overwhelming scientific evidence to the contrary, weakens confidence in science and diminishes the need for evidence. This seems reminiscent of Newspeak in Orwell's *1984* when there was no word for science. The American Association for the Advancement of Science and seventeen other leading scientific associations in the United States have clearly stated that not only is climate change occurring but that it is human induced[28].

Despite such overwhelming scientific evidence, many conservative politicians in the United States remain highly skeptical of climate change and have, on occasion, dismissed climate change as junk science[29].

Situations such as climate change denial make critical thinking skills more necessary than ever. The credibility of information cannot be assumed. Without a capacity for critical thinking, it will be too easy for future citizens to passively accept beliefs that lack any supporting evidence. The internet and social media have given misinformation and deception added potency. Social media also make democracies more vulnerable to interference from other countries.

In the United Kingdom, more than 150,000 Russian-based Twitter messages in English urged Britain to leave the European Union in the days before the referendum. Four hundred accounts identified as tools of the Russian Internet Research Agency pushed hard for Brexit, including divisive messages that sought to inflame fears about Muslims and immigrants[30].

In the United States, evidence that Russia attempted to interfere in the last U.S. election now seems inconvertible. An example of divisive interference would be the generation of 'Heart of Texas' Facebook posts by the Russian Internet Research Agency that aimed to inflame emotion over Muslim immigrants. Susceptible citizens readily pick up such posts, often adding their own incendiary comments. However, it seems that those same individuals will deny the true origin and intent of the initial posts even when given evidence of their origin[31].

Truth becomes unimportant when it is only one's view that counts and there is no interest in evidence. The inability or reluctance to think critically can only make electors more susceptible to manipulation making democracy more vulnerable.

What Can Be Done?

What can be done to equip citizens (and future citizens) to routinely judge the credibility and sources of information that shape their views? Defending democracy may need to begin in school to teach students to think for themselves instead of being passive recipients of other people's information. Concerns about critical thinking abilities of students have been identified in middle school and at university. For example, one study found that 82 percent of middle school students struggled to differentiate advertisements from real news stories even though the former had 'sponsored content' clearly labeled[32]. Similarly, a sample of (sophisticated?) university social science students were unable to distinguish fake news sites (including some such as the fake Boston Tribune that sounded as if it might be real) from real news sites[33]. Perhaps identifying fake news sources is not so easy.

So, should we be finding practical ways to help students think critically about the credibility of information outside the classroom as well as inside? Yes, according to California lawmakers[34] who have approved a bill requiring the Department of Education to provide media literacy resources and professional development programs for teachers to develop critical thinking skills.

There seems a consensus that critical thinking is an important aim of higher education with 89% of university teachers claiming critical thinking to be a primary objective of their instruction[35]. However, it seems that nearly half of college students may show no gain in critical thinking during their first two years and over one third show no gains after four years in college[36]. It has been suggested that promoting critical thinking skills is difficult[37] or not possible[38]. However, features of effective critical thinking programs have been identified[39]. The promotion of critical thinking is a fundamental aim of Philosophy for Children and shares features of programs that successfully promote critical thinking.

Placing critical thinking back in the context of democracy, Matthew Lipman[40] (p. 209) argued that democratic citizens need to think 'flexibly but responsibly. If they do not, they are prey for authoritarian and conformitarian propaganda'. In this sense, schools should be participatory communities where young people can develop as citizens[41] (p. 46). Philosophical inquiry provides a means of developing participatory communities and nurturing critical thinking. Critical thinking may help defend students not just against intentional misinformation and manipulation but also against inherent cognitive biases that further complicate the pursuit of truth.

Cognitive Biases Complicate 'Truth'

People who care about truth are likely to dismiss of the notion of 'alternative facts'. However, the belief that there is a strong concern among the broad populace for truth is likely to be incorrect. This belief stems from a cognitive bias termed the 'false consensus effect'[42], which refers to our tendency to overestimate the extent to which other people value what we value. The false consensus effect is one of several powerful 'cognitive biases' that can lead to people believing lies over truth.

Cognitive bias describes several demonstrable inherent thinking errors that we make in processing information. These thinking errors can prevent accurate understanding of *reality and truth*, even when confronted with the necessary data and *evidence* to form an accurate view. Our beliefs, judgments and understanding of the world rely heavily on previous experience and unconscious hidden inferences. The unconscious nature of our cognitive biases imply that we should be less certain in our judgments. We should also recognize that the views of other people that differ from our own may have more validity we think[43].

Confirmation bias is a cognitive bias that refers to our tendency to search for or interpret information in a way that confirms our preconceptions and discredit information that does not support these views. Confirmatory bias is particularly relevant to many instances described in this chapter. Cognitive biases influence the way we interpret situations and make judgments and decisions. They can lead us to erroneously attribute reasons why other people behave in certain ways, a bias known as 'fundamental attribution error'. Biases can also lead us to unconsciously and inaccurately stereotype other people. A classic example of stereotyping is the student Hannah in Darley and Gross's educational study[44].

Overcoming Bias

The scientific method places evidence behind an idea under open scrutiny and thus limits the consequences of bias and manipulation. Perhaps Orwell recognized this when his futuristic authoritarian society no longer had a word for science[6]. Misinformation is more likely to thrive when there is no appetite for supporting evidence. Further, it can be extremely difficult to change bias.

One strategy for combating misinformation is outlined in *The Truth-Seeker's Handbook*[45]. This approach provides guidelines to productively challenge people who deny facts. At the heart of this strategy is a recognition that emotions are much more powerful than reason.

For example, the rejection of climate change science and the vilification of immigrants have been based on the power to evoke feelings that give lies the same status as truth[8]. What is new is public susceptibility to misinformation and the ability of new technologies to manipulate and polarize opinion. When disputing fake information, we typically make the mistake of responding by presenting facts and arguing about evidence[45]. However, this is generally not effective in changing people's minds on charged issues. Confirmation bias can be very ingrained. In some cases, presenting the facts can actually cause people to develop a stronger attachment to their incorrect belief[46].

Attempts to influence a fact denier are likely to fail unless emotions are taken into account and a defensive or aggressive response avoided. The strategy's authors suggest that 'curious questioning', empathetic listening and building rapport are first necessary to establish shared goals with the denier[45]. Only once rapport has been achieved can facts held back in the beginning be effectively given in a final stage of the process. Emotions need to be addressed before any reasoned dialogue can take place. This process parallels the inquiry process in Philosophy for Children. The teacher's initial priority in facilitating inquiry is to establish an emotional climate in which students feel comfortable voicing their views and can 'hear' the views of others. Feeling comfortable is necessary before a reasoned discussion can take place that could lead a student can change their mind in the light of evidence.

Philosophical Ideas about Truth

When emotions matter more than facts, trust can readily evaporate and people create their separate realities, that is, their unsubstantiated beliefs. Creating our own realities is the core of relativism, the philosophical doctrine that knowledge, truth and morality are not absolute. If each of us knows only what we believe, there is no objective standard of truth and all moral positions become equally valid. Relativism contrasts with the central value of the Enlightenment that maintains truth is independent of opinion[47]. This latter position is consistent with the dialectical method used in philosophical inquiry. The dialectic is a discourse between two or more people holding different points of view about a subject but wishing to establish the truth through reasoned argument. This is the essence of philosophical inquiry as students support their views with reasons and disagree with reasons during discussion. Students strive for an objective standard of truth in contrast to passively accepting unsupported or biased opinion.

Concluding Comments on Participation and Democracy

An inquiry will not be productive unless the teacher seeks to engage students so they can participate in and contribute to discussion. The disposition to participate is also necessary for healthy democracies. It is also not possible to have a fully participative democratic society without an autonomous citizenry that can think, judge and act for themselves. Philosophy for Children has been advocated as an effective process of for nurturing critical thinking and wiser judgement[48].

This chapter has considered the contribution of classroom communities of inquiry to promoting citizens who are able and disposed to participate in and contributing to a healthy democracy. It has been argued that this is more important than ever in an age where information and misinformation are more readily available. The chapter has raised concerns about the ability of vested interests to manipulate the views and emotions of targeted individuals through social media and automated bots. Educating students to critically evaluate the credibility of large amounts of information available to them is seen as a potential antidote. Philosophical inquiry offers educators a process to help students search for truth using reason and good argument.

As H.G. Wells concluded in 1920 in the last pages of his epic *Outline of History*: 'Human history becomes more and more a race between education and catastrophe'[49] (Volume 2, p. 594). H.G. Wells is also reputed to have said 'Let us learn the truth and spread it as far and wide as our circumstances allow. For the truth is the greatest weapon we have'. This focus on the importance of truth provides an appropriate end to this chapter.

References

1. J. Dewey. The need of an industrial education in an industrial democracy. In J. A. Boydston (Ed.) *John Dewey, The middle works, 1899–1924 (Vol. 10, 1916–1917)*. 1980, pp. 137–143. Carbondale, IL: Southern Illinois University Press.
2. R. Keyes. *The post-truth era: Dishonesty and deception in contemporary life*. 2004. New York, NY: St Martin's Press.
3. Oxford Dictionaries. *Oxford dictionaries word of the year 2016 is...* 2016. Available at www.oxforddictionaries.com/press/news/2016/12/11/WOTY-16 [November 5, 2018].

4. Conway: Press Secretary gave alternative facts. *NBC News*. January 22, 2017. Available at: www.nbcnews.com/meet-the-press/video/conway-press-secretary-gave-alternative-facts-860142147643?v=raila& [November 7, 2018].

5. B. Zimmer. A clash of 'Alternative' and 'Facts': From the 16th century to a Trump counselor's phrase. *The Wall Street Journal*. January 26, 2017. Available at: www.wsj.com/articles/a-clash-of-alternative-and-facts-1485454691 [November 11, 2018].

6. G. Orwell. *1984*. 1949. London: Secker & Warburg (Penguin Random House).

7. Alternative facts. *Wikipedia*. Available at: https://en.wikipedia.org/wiki/Alternative_facts [November 2nd, 2018].

8. J. Seaton, T. Crook and D. J. Taylor. Welcome to dystopia – George Orwell experts on Donald Trump. *The Guardian*. January 25, 2017. Available at: www.theguardian.com/commentisfree/2017/jan/25/george-orwell-donald-trump-kellyanne-conway-1984 [November 1, 2018].

9. Giuliani vs. Chuck Todd: Truth isn't always truth, Comey's 'truth' different from Trump's 'truth'. *Realclear politics*. (Transcript of Meet the Press interview). August 19, 2018. Available at: www.realclearpolitics.com/video/2018/08/19/giuliani_truth_isnt_truth.html [November 2, 2018].

10. Fake news. In *Collins English Dictionary Complete and Unabridged Edition (13th Edition)*. 2018. Glasgow, UK: HarperCollins. Available at: www.collinsdictionary.com/us/dictionary/english/fake-news [November 2, 2018].

11. The White House. *Remarks by President Obama and Chancellor Merkel in joint press conference*. April 24, 2016. Available at: https://obamawhitehouse.archives.gov/the-press-office/2016/04/24/remarks-president-obama-and-chancellor-merkel-joint-press-conference [November 3, 2018].

12. President Obama farewell speech full text. *CNN*. January 10, 2017. Available at: www.cnn.com/2017/01/10/politics/president-obama-farewell-speech/index.html [November 1, 2018].

13. S. Tavernise. As fake news spreads lies, more readers shrug at the truth. *New York Times*, December 6, 2016. Available at: www.nytimes.com/2016/12/06/us/fake-news-partisan-republican-democrat.html [November 1, 2018].

14. Computational propaganda: Bots, targeting and the future. *NPR radio station.* February 9, 2018. Available at: www.npr.org/sections/13.7/2018/02/09/584514805/computational-propaganda-yeah-that-s-a-thing-now [November 3, 2018].

15. H. Allcott and M. Gentzkow. Social media and fake news in the 2016 Election. *Journal of Economic Perspectives,* 2017, vol. 31, issue 2, pp. 211–236.

16. J. Diamond. Trump: 'I'm afraid the election's going to be rigged'. *CNN.* August 2, 2016. Available at: www.cnn.com/2016/08/01/politics/donald-trump-election-2016-rigged/index.html [November 5, 2018].

17. S. Shane. From headline to photograph, a fake news masterpiece. *New York Times,* January 18, 2017. Available at: www.nytimes.com/2017/01/18/us/fake-news-hillary-clinton-cameron-harris.html [November 3, 2018].

18. J. Coscarelli. Kellyanne Conway admits 'Bowling Green Massacre' error. *New York Times,* February 3, 2017. Available at: www.nytimes.com/2017/02/03/us/politics/bowling-green-massacre-kellyanne-conway.html [November 2, 2018].

19. A. Blake. Kellyanne Conway's 'Bowling Green massacre' wasn't a slip of the tongue. She has said it before. *The Washington Post,* February 6, 2017. Available at: www.washingtonpost.com/news/the-fix/wp/2017/02/06/kellyanne-conways-bowling-green-massacre-wasnt-a-slip [November 2, 2018].

20. S. Vosoughi, D. Roy and S. Aral. The spread of true and false news online. *Science,* 2018, vol. 359, issue 6380, pp. 1146–1151.

21. A. Quigley. Who is Alex Jones? His top five conspiracy theories ahead of Megyn Kelly's interview. *Newsweek,* June 6, 2017. Available at: www.newsweek.com/who-alex-jones-his-top-five-conspiracy-theories-ahead-nbc-megyn-kelly-626633 [November 1, 2018].

22. D. Arkin and B. Popken. How the internet's conspiracy theorists turned Parkland students into 'crisis actors'. *NBC News,* February 21, 2018. Available at: www.nbcnews.com/news/us-news/how-internet-s-conspiracy-theorists-turned-parkland-students-crisis-actors-n849921 [November 3, 2018].

23. L. Sydell. We tracked down a fake-news creator in the suburbs. Here's what we learned. *NPR,* November 23, 2016. Available at: www.npr.org/sections/alltechconsidered/2016/11/23/503146770/

npr-finds-the-head-of-a-covert-fake-news-operation-in-the-suburbs [November 2, 2018].

24. V. Narayanan et al. *Polarization, partisanship and junk news consumption over social media in the US. Data Memo 2018.1.* Oxford, UK: Project on Computational Propaganda.

25. Hiram Johnson. In Wikiquote. 2018. Available at: https://en.wikiquote.org/wiki/Hiram_Johnson [November 2, 2018].

26. M. Bowden. *Hue 1968: A turning point of the American War in Vietnam.* 2017. New York, NY: Atlantic Monthly Press.

27. J. Stone. Nearly half of Britons believe Vote Leave's false '£350 million a week to the EU' claim. *The Independent*, June 16, 2016. Available at: www.independent.co.uk/news/uk/politics/nearly-half-of-britons-believe-vote-leaves-false-350-million-a-week-to-the-eu-claim-a7085016.html [November 3, 2018].

28. American Association for the Advancement of Science. *AAAS reaffirms statements on climate change and integrity.* December 4, 2009. Available at: www.aaas.org/news/aaas-reaffirms-statements-climate-change-and-integrity [February 4, 2019].

29. R. E. Dunlop and A. M. McCright. Organized climate change denial. In J. S. Dryzek, R. B. Norgaard and D. Schlosberg (Eds.), *The Oxford handbook of climate change and society.* 2011, pp. 144–160. Oxford, England: University Press.

30. R. Booth et al. Russia used hundreds of fake accounts to tweet about Brexit, data show. *The Guardian*, November 14, 2017. Available at: www.theguardian.com/world/2017/nov/14/how-400-russia-run-fake-accounts-posted-bogus-brexit-tweets [November 3, 2018].

31. S. Shane and M. Mazzetti. The plot to subvert an election: Unravelling the Russia story so far. *New York Times (Special Report)*, September 20, 2018, pp. F1–F11.

32. S. Wineburg et al. Evaluating information: The cornerstone of civic online reasoning. *Stanford Digital Repository*, 2016. Available at: http://purl.stanford.edu/fv751yt5934 [November 2, 2018].

33. D. Stecula. Fake news might be harder to spot than most people believe. *The Washington Post*, July 10, 2017. Available at: www.washingtonpost.com/news/monkey-cage/wp/2017/07/10/fake-news-might-be-harder-to-spot-than-most-people-believe/?utm_term=.d17318284b7a [November 3, 2018].

34. S. Minichiello. California lawmakers advance bill to help teens combat fake news. *The Press Democrat*, September 2, 2018.

Available at: www.pressdemocrat.com/news/8689637-181/california-lawmakers-advance-bill-to?sba=AAS [November 3, 2018].

35. R. W. Paul, L. Elder and T. Bartell. *California teacher preparation for instruction in critical thinking: Research findings and policy recommendations.* 1997. Tomales, CA: Foundation for Critical Thinking.

36. R. Arum and J. Roks. *Academically adrift: Limited learning on college campuses.* 2011. Chicago, IL: University of Chicago Press.

37. D. T. Willingham. Critical thinking: Why is it so hard to teach? *American Educator*, Summer 2007, pp. 8–19.

38. M. J. Adler. Critical thinking programs: Why they won't work. *Education Digest*, 1987, vol. 52, issue 7, p. 9.

39. P. C. Abrami. Instructional interventions affecting critical thinking skills and dispositions: A stage 1 meta-analysis. *Review of Educational Research*, 2008, vol. 78, issue 4, pp. 275–314.

40. M. Lipman. *Thinking in education.* 2003. Cambridge, England: Cambridge University Press.

41. J. Haynes. *Children as philosophers.* 2002. New York, NY: RoutledgeFalmer.

42. False consensus effect. *Wikipedia.* 2018. Available at: https://en.wikipedia.org/wiki/False_consensus_effect [November 3, 2018].

43. R. E. Nisbett. *Mindware: Tools for smart thinking.* 2015. New York, NY: Farrer, Straus and Giroux.

44. J. M. Darley and P. H. Gross. A hypothesis-confirming bias in labeling effects. *Journal of Personality and Social Psychology*, 1983, vol. 44, issue 1, pp. 20–33.

45. G. Tsipursky and L. Holliday. *The truth-seeker's handbook: A science-based guide.* 2017. Columbus, OH: Intentional Insights Press.

46. G. J. Trevors et al. Identity and epistemic emotions during knowledge revision: A potential account for the backfire effect. *Discourse Processes*, 2016, vol. 53, issue 5–6, pp. 339–370.

47. M. D'Ancona. *Post-truth: The new war on truth and how to fight back.* 2017. London: Ebury Press (Penguin Random House).

48. R. Fisher. *Teaching thinking: Philosophical enquiry in the classroom.* 1998. London: Cassell.

49. H. G. Wells. *Outline of history.* 1920. London: George Newnes. Available at: www.gutenberg.org/files/45368/45368-h/45368-h.htm [November 2, 2018].

11

Lessons Learned in Sustaining and Embedding

At the beginning of a project on the Civil War, one teacher began with an excerpt from a story about the murder of the wife of one of the main characters by a soldier. The students were 10 years old and had already spent six months practicing philosophical inquiry. They formulated philosophical questions (as in Stage 2 in Chapter 3) and had an inquiry. The teacher reported that the enthusiasm for the project seemed to be heightened by this beginning, and although thereafter it proceeded along more traditional teaching lines, there nevertheless remained a high level of questioning by the students and an openness to exploring different lines of thinking. Some three years later, when the students were in high school, a group of them were observed in a history class. The lesson was to do with reasons for invasions and one girl tried valiantly (three times) to offer alternative ideas and open up the discussion. Each time the teacher refused to deviate from the accepted 'facts' and finally told the girl to 'Be quiet!' This shows the importance of a 'joined up' approach to inquiry!

What You Need to Do

Even while the students are in your own class, you will need to think about continuing review, feedback and injection of further novelty and enthusiasm. Most projects need some rejuvenation after a few weeks or months – just small changes to inject novelty and provide new oxygen. If you don't do this, all your students will not automatically keep going and maintain the use of their skills. This is also true of the teachers – they need some variation to spice up their teaching life as well! Publicizing your project inside or outside school might expand subsequent recruitment or attract additional funding – but should make you and the kids feel good anyway. Once the students go to the classes of other teachers, this becomes even more important.

While you have the students in your class, you might work on having them consciously broaden their new skills to different materials and contexts for new purposes. This will consolidate the progress made, build confidence and empower students still further. Try to prepare the students for the situation in other classes where the teachers may not be sympathetic to the process of P4C. How could they handle this situation? This is a good topic for an inquiry!

Starting a project can be very demanding in terms of time and energy, although that investment is almost always considered worthwhile later. Once things are up and running smoothly, it is tempting to either relax or rush on and start another project with a different group. The latter is more dangerous than the former – don't spread yourself too thinly. Better to do a few things well than many things badly.

Teachers have unique knowledge of their own schools and teaching conditions. All Philosophy for Children needs adjustment to the local characteristics of classrooms. Beyond this, enthusiastic teachers often want to customize or adapt methods, to 'suit' their own classroom or children. However, a word of warning is needed. Only the structured methods described here have been evaluated. If you customize so enthusiastically that your method no longer bears much relationship to the original, you cannot expect automatic transfer of effectiveness. For all of these reasons, we suggest that – at least for your first venture into this field – you keep to the guidelines outlined in this book (which still needs you to make many professional decisions about what is best for your own class and your own children).

Many teachers will worry about the neediest children, whether their neediness arises from a continuing learning disability, from a more transient learning problem or from cultural or language difficulties. Will such children be able to do philosophy? Sometimes teachers are tempted to exclude such children from a project. We do not recommend this. All children should have the opportunity to participate in and benefit from

Philosophical Inquiry. Even your weakest students can learn! The fact that they are required to interact will certainly place demands upon them, and these demands will help them to learn. We often find that it is students who were formerly perceived as less able who flourish in inquiry lessons.

Teachers spend every working day as part of a busy community – yet all-too-often feel strangely isolated. Finding time together to have a discussion about anything is difficult enough – and at the end of the school day, energies are at a low ebb for professional discussions. Ideally, time should be scheduled to bring teachers together regularly in mutual support and problem-solving gatherings where they can share their ideas, materials and methods – and build each other's confidence and self-esteem. Teachers learn most effectively from each other by sharing their experiences in implementing innovative practice. A first step in this direction would be to invite a colleague to your philosophy session, and then ask their opinion – about good points and then points for possible improvement. Another good resource could be keeping in touch with other schools that use philosophy. Maybe teachers can visit each other's school and observe philosophy sessions to learn how other colleagues do it and compare notes on implementation. Exchanging experiences between students could be interesting too. If schools are not near each other, you can use the internet and create a network to share the projects and learn from each other, perhaps including video clips of each other's practice for comment by the other school. This is a kind of peer learning, when the peers are whole schools as well as individuals.

Habits and Dispositions

Aristotle is reputed to have said: 'We are what we repeatedly do. Excellence, then, is not an act but a habit.' (While this quotation is usually attributed to Aristotle[1] it is actually a paraphrasing by Will Durant[2]). To truly be a critical thinker the student needs to do more than justify an opinion during an inquiry. The student needs to develop the *habit* of thinking critically in a variety of circumstances over time. Independent thinking is a disposition as well as a skill. Similarly, the practice of inquiry needs to become embedded in classroom practice, not be just a one-off activity that quickly fades. By developing habits and dispositions, the thinker goes some way towards proofing themselves against the many changes of circumstances that await them. Sustaining philosophical inquiry in the classroom is far from straightforward in educational contexts riven with competing demands and pressures. Many innovations in education (even when evidence-based) come and go as teachers and their enthusiasms change.

Cost-Effectiveness

In the strategic allocation of scarce resources, the question of cost-effectiveness remains pertinent. Cognitive interventions are a more cost-effective way of improving learning outcomes than many other approaches often automatically thought to improve classroom performance. An investigation[3] of the effect-size of 33 factors associated with achievement identified the student's cognitive ability as having the second largest effect (after formative feedback) on student learning. This is consistent with the finding[4] of the strong relationship between cognitive ability at 11 years and national test results at age 16. Cost-effective cognitive interventions are likely to have a positive effect on long-term learning outcomes.

Philosophy for Children is an example of a cost-effective cognitive intervention[5,6]. The largest cost is likely to be incurred through training teachers in how to facilitate inquiries. Training in the Scottish study amounted to US$16 per participating student. In the Education Endowment Foundation study, the cost to deliver the project in one school for one academic year was approximately $23 per student, as they chose to hire external consultants. In subsequent years, costs decrease as trained teachers work with new cohorts of children. This compares favorably with other educational programs that may not have empirical support for effectiveness.

Cautionary Tales: Sustaining over Time

Although the cost-effectiveness of philosophical inquiry is encouraging, teacher excitement needs to be tempered by the realities of working with competing priorities, deadlines and expectations. The experience gained from previous studies[5] suggests that Philosophy for Children works best when space is dedicated in the curriculum, ideally as a discrete subject, Philosophy. Otherwise, the pressure of narrow testable objectives makes it difficult for teacher and students to think together and explore issues in depth. Such pressures reinforce a more traditional teacher-student communication pattern that tends to close down discussion. When an hour of P4C is taken as a weekly activity, rationally time can be taken from other subjects because aspects of that subject are effectively done through the philosophy session and the skills learned when applied to different subjects make learning more effective. There are obvious curricular targets like English, social studies and religious studies, but all subject areas could contribute.

However, philosophical inquiry makes no pretense of offering a simple panacea. What it does offer is a process and structure to gradually develop student thinking over time. Inquiry enables 'thinking in the moment' and allows spontaneous (and satisfying) exchanges freely exploring ideas. Inquiry thus provides an alternative to direct, targeted instruction and offers an antidote to more rigid repetitive practice. The method can be infused into the teaching of other subjects alongside more traditional teaching approaches – that of course still continue to be necessary. Inquiry is demanding for both teacher and students and would probably be exhausting if it was the teacher's only approach to learning. It is better seen as a powerful extra tool in the teachers' armory of strategies.

We have noted that benefits from inquiry (and some other thinking programs) tend to gradually build over time. However, this gradual accumulation of gains may be too slow if curricular pressures demand evidence of quick (if superficial) learning. Unless teacher colleagues, parents and the wider public understand the importance of critical thinking, individual teachers are in danger of finding themselves swimming against a strong tide. Teachers need continuing, good-quality training to sustain classroom dialogue, but also to have the confidence to persist with the support of their managers.

Students who become adept at posing good questions in elementary school can be perceived as inappropriate in high school if teachers are unfamiliar with independently thinking students. Teachers may be concerned that they are giving up some control when they encourage students to freely express their views (even if with respect). The teacher's perception of their role as behavior managers may conflict with encouraging student questioning and listening carefully to what students are saying. It is a different pedagogy. The classroom model of behavior control moves from one of being external (i.e., the teacher) to internal (i.e., self-governance). We have seen students in a P4C lesson telling another student they were not willing to put up with her disruptive behavior since they wanted to pursue the inquiry. Peer pressure is powerful and effective!

This book has noted in Chapter 6 that exercising reasoning is effortful and tends not to be the brain's first choice[7]. Our inbuilt unconscious tendency toward reacting instinctively and emotionally tends to outweigh thoughtful responses unless students have been schooled otherwise. Automatic heuristics prevail despite 'higher', more complex cognitive processes that produce better outcomes in the longer term. A range of pedagogical, organizational and biological factors may thus mitigate against sustaining philosophical inquiry across school systems. Innovative practice can threaten the professional self-esteem of managers or colleagues who do not fully understand the process and benefits of inquiry methods. Managers and colleagues have the potential to support or inadvertently (or intentionally) sabotage the fledgling developments of teachers inquiring with students.

Teachers are more likely to make a long-term commitment to inquiry when they are given sustained positive encouragement, have parents onboard, receive support at the school district level and when there has been positive publicity in local or national media. However, sustaining innovative cognitive practices beyond their initial success can be a different matter. Studies based on interviews with teachers[8] suggest that only in a few cases would cognitive innovations survive the departure of key members of staff.

In the Thinking Through Philosophy program in Scotland, when key teachers retired or gained promotion to posts in different schools, when the original trainers were no longer available and when a particularly supportive school superintendent was no longer in their post things began to fall apart. Momentum is easily lost if organizational energy is not maintained at the school and district level and where support from credible teacher 'champions' has been discontinued. Even in these circumstances, there will always be individual teachers sufficiently committed to inquiry to maintain quality practice well after the completion of a project. But to build greater depth and expand to more teachers, it does seem a local champion is needed.

Lipman's initial hope was that philosophy would become part of the K–12 curriculum[9]. Perhaps the best introduction would be if it were embedded in initial teacher training – that way it becomes part of the 'default mode' returned to by teachers even while pressured by the passing whims and fashions of curricular change. While adherents of Philosophy for Children might enthusiastically wish this to be the case, several factors have been noted in this chapter that can work against this. Inserting something in initial teacher education means displacing something else – and few ITE teachers are willing to give up their precious topic. 'Top-down' reform needs very careful management if resistance from teachers more wedded to traditional practices is to be avoided. Training in continuing professional development requires a credible, organized and funded program. As suggested in Chapter 1, the success of any educational initiative ultimately depends on the enthusiasm, commitment and creativity of teachers who are involved in actual engagement with students.

Thought also needs to be given to how developments in elementary schools can best be extended to high schools (and indeed developments in nurseries and kindergartens extended to primary schools). In the upper reaches of education, classes may be organized differently with less of a 'whole child' ethos and a more fragmented subject-oriented view of education. Despite organizational differences between elementary, middle and high schools, philosophical inquiry can be infused into a wide range of subjects and this then increases the feasibility of using it.

This infusing goes beyond just having formal inquiries within a subject area, although these can be an excellent tool in widening thinking and exploring aspects of any subject. For example, keeping in mind the philosophical inquiry elements of cognitive challenge, social construction and metacognition, one high school science teacher decided to be innovative. Instead of proceeding with a traditional lesson she asked the class not to speak or comment but just observe. She then demonstrated a short experiment. After a couple of minutes of 'thinking time' she asked students to consider what had been happening. Then, in small groups they were asked to formulate questions to explore their understanding of what had been observed during the experiment. As a class they then asked questions. Later, for the metacognitive aspect, they had to consider how well they had done and what evidence was there for their views. How could they do better next time? For example, better attention? More insightful questions? At the end, they seemed to have a good knowledge of acids and alkalis – the subject of the lesson – and they enjoyed the process!

Skills for the World

Philosophy for Children is not just for the United States or not even just for English-speaking countries. It has been used in over 60 countries around the world, including developing countries where you might imagine the children's thoughts are on where the next food is coming from rather than philosophy. But philosophical inquiry has been shown to be adaptable across the world in different social and curricular contexts – and in different economic, cultural and linguistic contexts.

Stimuli that reflect local contexts are important when first introducing P4C. Others that bring new ideas and broaden the horizons of students may be more usefully added when there is more familiarity with the method. At the start of the project to introduce Thinking Through Philosophy in Grenada, the only story book at elementary school level that could be found in the local government bookshop was the Ladybird version of Heidi – a story from Switzerland! The project leaders brought copies of Caribbean Traditional Tales and used these, along with stories from the internet and also a poem by a local teacher, to have stimuli that better resonated with local culture. In India, the traditional Panchatantra stories were used, which were readily available on the internet. In a project in South Africa, the concept of Ubuntu (our common humanity and unity) was explored through P4C. The method is adaptable to the United States, the United Kingdom, the Caribbean, India, Africa or anywhere else.

Skills for the Future

Claxton[10] suggested that the only thing we can say with confidence about the future is that there is not much we can say about it with confidence. Therefore, he argued, the only sensible role of education is to get students ready to cope with complexity, uncertainty and ambiguity – so they can craft a satisfying life in this context. Coping with uncertainty and ambiguity requires pedagogies and practices that place more emphasis on independent thinking. The previous knowledge-based certainties of teachers are less relevant in an age where information is freely available and the main challenge is how to apply that knowledge in real-life situations. Classroom 'communities of inquiry' encourage teachers to model dispositions such as curiosity that are necessary to deal with this increased uncertainty and ambiguity. Such communities contribute to developing student capacities as successful learners, confident individuals and responsible citizens.

Curricula may need to be rethought to create space for practicing thinking, communicating and collaborative problem-solving. Otherwise, most people, most of the time, will come to quick conclusions without fully taking into account the evidence[11]. Excessive curricular content needs to be reduced (or 'de-cluttered') to increase opportunities for students to think together. The aspirational goals of successful learners, confident individuals and responsible citizens cannot be achieved through traditional instruction alone. They require more emphasis on students' constructing and creating meaning and understanding through discussion and dialogue with others.

All of this requires teachers to be creative and courageous in thinking about the curriculum. However, the strength of P4C is its versatility. For example, even in outdoor education the method can be used. A group of students were engaged in various outdoor activities that challenged them to think. A group were given some planks of timber and a couple of crates. Parallel ropes laid on the ground delineated a river, which was notionally filled with alligators. The task was to get all students and the equipment across the river without anyone falling prey to an alligator. It was the approach that was different from the norm, which emphasized the thinking aspect. First, the students had a dialogue to put forward various solutions. These options had to be examined and evidence for the efficacy of each put forward. Next the children tried out the preferred solution. Then had more discussion on their efforts and how they could do things better. They left a 'top tip' for the next group. This basic coherence between different aspects of the curriculum further built the skills and dispositions of the students.

Views of what makes a 'good' teacher are also relevant to any realignment of future classroom interactions. Teachers increasingly emphasize personal qualities (such as enthusiasm, adaptability, openness, creativity and resilience) over their subject knowledge[12]. Students seem to agree with their teachers as to what makes a good teacher[13,14]. Students value teachers who listen, allow students to have their say and care about students' opinions. Students' emphasis on 'soft' interpersonal skills does not undermine their view of the importance of teachers having high expectations and challenging young people to do better. The qualities identified that make a good teacher are necessary for supporting communities of inquiry.

Changes in perceptions of practice are reflected in widespread agreement[14] with the notion of the teacher becoming more of an enabler, facilitator or learning manager. The shift to the teacher as facilitator rather than 'instructor' is consistent with the pedagogy and practice of philosophical inquiry. Communities of inquiry are consistent with, and supportive of, educational practice that equips students to manage in a society driven by continuous change.

Final Thoughts

Assuming you have now read all the book (in whatever order), take a moment to reflect on your learning journey. How good did you think you were before you read this book? Have you implemented some of its suggestions? How good do you think you are now? Where will you go next and how good are you going to be in the future? Well, if you are that good, you might want to become an in-service training leader....

A Teacher's Guide to Philosophy for Children has described a process for teaching students of all ages to think and reason together so that they can, in turn, think for themselves. This process extends their thinking and understanding beyond that which they could achieve individually. The whole is truly greater than the sum of the parts. Students become more adept at make informed choices through collaborative dialogue. Exploring philosophical questions of interest to the students contributes to their cognitive and social development and, in so doing, prepares them for dealing with the uncertainties of the future. Equally important, inquiring with students and searching for meaning and truth feeds their curiosity. Returning to the opening quote in the first chapter, the philosophical inquiry process contributes to students retaining their curiosity, imagination and creativity as they continue along their path of lifelong learning. Educators need to be working and walking with them on that journey.

References

1. Aristotle. *Ethics*, ii, 4, *The Nicomachean ethics*. 2004. London: Penguin Classics.
2. W. Durant. *The story of philosophy: The lives and opinions of the world's greatest philosophers. Part VII: Ethics and the nature of happiness*. 1926, p. 87. New York, NY: Simon & Schuster.

3. J. Hattie. *Teachers make a difference: What is the research evidence?* Australian Council for Educational Research Annual Conference Building Teacher Quality. University of Auckland, October 2003. Available: https://research.acer.edu.au/cgi/viewcontent.cgi?article= 1003&context=research_conference_2003 [12 November 2018].

4. I. J. Deary et al., Intelligence and educational achievement. *Intelligence*, 2007, vol. 35, issue 1, pp. 13–21.

5. S. Gorard, N. Siddiqui and B. H. See. Can Philosophy for Children improve primary school attainment? *Journal of Philosophy of Education*, February 2017, vol. 51, issue 1, pp. 5–22.

6. S. Trickey and K. J. Topping. Philosophy for Children: A systematic review. *Research Papers in Education*, 2004, vol. 19, issue 3, pp. 363–378.

7. D. Kahneman. *Thinking, fast and slow.* 2011. New York, NY: Farrer, Straus & Giroux.

8. D. Leat. Rolling the stone uphill: Teacher development and the implementation of thinking skills programmes. *Oxford Review of Education*, September 1999, vol. 25 no. 3, pp. 387–403.

9. M. Lipman, A. M. Sharp and F. Oscanyon. *Philosophy in the classroom*, 1980, p. 51. Philadelphia, PA: Temple University Press.

10. G. L. Claxton. *Building learning power: Helping young people become better learners.* 2002. Bristol, England: TLO Ltd.

11. D. Perkins. Postprimary education has little impact on informal reasoning. *Journal of Educational Psychology*, 1985, vol. 77, pp. 562–571.

12. P. Rudd, M. Rickinson and P. Benefield. *Mapping work on the future of teaching and learning. Final report for the general teaching council*, 2004. Slough, England: National Foundation of Educational Research & General Teaching Council for England.

13. J. MacBeath. *Schools must speak for themselves: The case for school self-evaluation*, 1999. London: RoutledgeFalmer.

14. C. Day. *A passion for teaching.* 2004, p. 40. London: RoutledgeFalmer.

Index

Made in the USA
Columbia, SC
17 August 2024

40589863R00104